MW00453031

# Old Santa Fe Today

Simon Nusbaum House. Destruction of this
building on the southeast corner of Washington
Avenue and Nusbaum Street for a municipal
parking lot in 1960 provided the impetus for the
establishment of The Historic Santa Fe Foundation
in 1961.
*David W. Matthews, photographer*

# Old Santa Fe Today

*Fourth Edition*

Preface by John Gaw Meem
Note to the Third Edition by M. R. (Jim) Adler
Note to the Fourth Edition by Stephen E. Watkins

Published for The Historic Santa Fe Foundation
by the University of New Mexico Press
Albuquerque

© 1991 by The Historic Santa Fe Foundation.
All rights reserved.
*Fourth Edition.*
Manufactured in the United States of America
Library of Congress Catalog Number 191-12114
International Standard Book Number 0-8263-1303-5
First edition © 1966 by The School of American
   Research
Second edition © 1972 by The Historic Santa Fe
   Foundation
Third edition © 1982 by The Historic Santa Fe
   Foundation

**Library of Congress Cataloging in Publication Data**
Main entry under title:

Old Santa Fe today/preface by John Gaw Meem.
   —4th ed./note to the fourth edition by Stephen
   E. Watkins.
      p.    cm.
      ISBN 0–8263–1303–5

   1. Historic buildings—New Mexico—Santa Fe—
Guide–books.   2. Architecture—New Mexico—
Santa Fe—Guide–books.   3. Santa Fe (N.M.)—History.   4. Santa Fe (N.M.)—Buildings, structures,
etc.—Guide–books.   5. Santa Fe (N.M.)—Description—Guide–books.   I. Historic Santa Fe
Foundation.
F804.S28A27    1992
978.9'56—dc20                              91–12114
                                                CIP

## Acknowledgments

To *The New Mexican* for permission to use certain portions of its copyrighted series "Let's Keep Our
Heritage."

To the State of New Mexico Records Center for the
assistance of the staff of its Division of Historical Services and its archival facilities.

To the Museum of New Mexico for the assistance of
its research personnel and staff photographer.

To the Avery-Bowman Abstract Company and the Santa
Fe Abstract and Title Company Incorporated for research assistance and use of property records.

To the owners of historic homes and buildings in Santa
Fe who have permitted the structures included in this
book to be photographed and described.

COVER: ROQUE TUDESQUI HOUSE, entrance gate with
wisteria, 135 East de Vargas.
*Mark Nohl, photographer*

# Contents

◊ A shield indicates that The Historic Santa Fe Foundation has placed a bronze plaque on this building to designate it as being worthy of preservation.
Buildings capitalized within text are featured in this book.

# Preface

This book had its origin in a small pamphlet published by The Historic Santa Fe Foundation in 1962 entitled *Historic Buildings & Sites of Santa Fe*. Some of the material was later expanded into a series of articles, "Let's Keep Our Heritage," which appeared from time to time in *The New Mexican*, the local newspaper that has consistently backed the movement for the preservation of Santa Fe's historical assets. The series was edited by me and sponsored by the Old Santa Fe Association, with documentation furnished by The Historic Santa Fe Foundation.

These two organizations are at the heart of the movement for preserving the city's cultural heritage of historic and architecturally significant buildings. It is appropriate, however, to note that it was due to the generosity and foresight of historically minded citizens in former years that Santa Fe still has SENA PLAZA, restored by Miss Amelia E. White and others; the ARIAS DE QUIROS buildings, preserved by Mrs. William B. Field; and EL ZAGUÁN and the BORREGO HOUSE, preserved by Mrs. Margretta S. Dietrich.

The Old Santa Fe Association is the older organization, founded in 1926 with the avowed objective:

> To preserve and maintain the ancient landmarks, historical structures, and traditions of Old Santa Fe, to guide its growth and development in such a way as to sacrifice as little as possible of that unique charm, born of age, tradition and environment which are the priceless assets and heritage of Old Santa Fe.

It has been at the forefront of every fight for conservation since then. Sometimes it has lost, as in the case of the Nusbaum Building, a fine example of Territorial architecture that was torn down by the city to make way for a parking lot, and the Curry House at the west end of the BARRIO DE ANALCO, which was demolished as a result of the Urban Renewal project.

But the association has often won, notably in its fight for the adoption of the city's Historic Zoning Ordinance, which protects the distinctive character of the historic area of Santa Fe by requiring that new construction harmonize with the old. This ordinance was drawn up by the Hon. Samuel Z. Montoya, at the time Santa Fe city attorney, later justice of the state supreme court, and members of the city planning commission, Irene von Horvath and the late Oliver La Farge. In a landmark victory in the struggle for historic preservation, the ordinance has been declared constitutional by the state supreme court.

The Historic Santa Fe Foundation was founded in 1961 to receive tax-exempt donations, to administer property, and to engage in educational and research activities. Since then it has placed bronze plaques on twenty-nine buildings in Santa Fe and its environs that, as the result of its documented research, were deemed worthy of preservation. In addition, it played an important role in having most of these (as well as others) placed on the State Register of Cultural Properties, from which several have been selected for designation as National Historic Landmarks. The Historic Santa Fe Foundation is currently administering, through a contractual agreement with the owner, the LORETTO CHAPEL, one of the properties it worked diligently to help preserve.

A tax-exempt organization such as The Historic Santa Fe Foundation is needed because gifts, both large and small, are required to save endangered historic and other significant buildings from destruction; and because the Old Santa Fe Association frequently must work to influence legislation on behalf of its objectives, it cannot receive or participate in tax-exempt donations.

The buildings and sites chosen for inclusion in both the original publication and in this revised and expanded edition were selected by the Board of Directors of The Historic Santa Fe Foundation as recommended by members of its Historic Research Committee. Those responsible for the research and writing of the texts for the items in this book include: Mrs. Lief Ericson Mueller, researcher; Mrs. Gertrude Hill Muir, formerly Librarian of the Museum of New Mexico, now a member of the Library staff of Arizona State University, Tempe, Arizona; Mrs. Sylvia G. Loomis, formerly Executive Secretary for both The Historic Santa Fe Foundation and the Old Santa Fe Association, now on the staff of the Archives of American Art, who edited the text of the first edition; J. D. Sena, Jr., and Boyd Cockrell of the Santa Fe Abstract and Title Company, Inc.; Bruce T. Ellis, former Curator of History of the Museum of New Mexico; Alan C. Vedder, Conservator for the Museum of New Mexico; E. Boyd, Curator Emeritus of the Spanish Colonial Arts Department of the Museum of New Mexico, and Myra Ellen Jenkins, State Historian and member of the staff of the New Mexico State Records Center, who was also responsible for the editing of this edition.

Publication of *Old Santa Fe Today* has been supported by the School of American Research. Founded in 1907 and quartered in Santa Fe since 1909, the school has a distinguished record of achievement in field archaeology and anthropological research. Its participation in the 1912 remodeling of the PALACE OF THE GOVERNORS helped to establish the local regional style: the long portal on the PLAZA was reconstructed in a manner authentic to the traditions of the Santa Fe area. The school has conducted archaeological excavations at such major southwestern sites as Chaco Canyon and Bandelier National Monument, and its four-year archaeological project within and on the North Rim of the Grand Canyon (1967–70) was the first systematic inquiry into early man's occupation and use of this great natural land feature. Its many scholarly professional seminars continue to bring credit to the Santa Fe community. The Board of The Historic Santa Fe Foundation acknowledges with appreciation the action of the Board of Managers of the School of American Research in making possible the inclusion of *Old Santa Fe Today* among the many distinguished publications in the school's long history.

The coordination between The Historic Santa Fe Foundation and the School of American Research has been under the direction of Milton R. Adler, immediate past chairman of the Foundation and one of its founders. Peter Dechert, former Assistant Director of the School of American Research, has assisted in all matters concerning this publication.

The entire project has been one of cooperation on the part of many individuals, devoted to the task of recording and preserving the architecture, traditions, and history of Old Santa Fe. It is their hope that this book will move others to help Santa Fe keep its character and individuality by supporting the organization dedicated to this purpose.

John Gaw Meem
October 1972

# Note to the Third Edition

By 1966 when the School of American Research published The Historic Santa Fe Foundation's first edition of *Old Santa Fe Today*, the Foundation was five years old, and had placed its shield-shaped **WORTHY OF PRESERVATION** plaques on sixteen of the thirty-three buildings and sites covered in that book. In 1972, with the close cooperation of the School of American Research, the Foundation brought forth through its new publisher, the University of New Mexico Press, the revised and enlarged second edition of *Old Santa Fe Today*. By then, twenty-three of the forty-one properties bore the Foundation's preservation plaque. In this further revised and enlarged third edition, forty-one of the fifty-five properties covered have been researched and plaqued by the Foundation through this, its twentieth, year.

For its first ten years The Historic Santa Fe Foundation was very busy establishing itself through fulfilling the educational and research portions of its mission. In 1962 it produced its first publication, a pamphlet entitled *Historic Buildings & Sites of Santa Fe*. This pamplet, which sold for 10¢, was reprinted twice before it was expanded into the first edition of *Old Santa Fe Today*. By this time the Foundation had also begun the ongoing activity of documenting and plaquing properties, and, where applicable, requesting their placement on the state and national registers of historic properties. In addition, it began to hold open houses for Foundation members and to conduct guided tours for the public of selected historic homes; sponsor and conduct the annual Traditional Christmas Lighting Contest; address service club and chamber of commerce luncheons on the importance of historic preservation; publish periodic newsletters for the membership [this developed into the bulletin that the Foundation continues to publish and mail quarterly]; conduct membership drives; and generally promote the cause of historic preservation wherever possible, on its own or in cooperation with others.

During the past ten years the Foundation initiated a change in both the direction and scope of its work. This change began slowly, then accelerated to today's almost hectic pace that finds the Foundation becoming increasingly involved in more and more of the various aspects of the multifaceted field that is historic preservation. The first step in this change was the acceptance by the Foundation of a generous contract offer from the new owners of the LORETTO CHAPEL to administer it in return for a fee.

The most significant decision made by the Foundation was to purchase and restore the PINCKNEY R. TULLY HOUSE in 1973, thus saving it from demolition for a parking lot. By early 1974 the purchase was completed. To do this, the Foundation had to augment its own relatively meager funds through public and private donations, loans, matching city, state, and federal grant money, and a lease negotiated with the tenants that provided for their restoring the building's interior under the Foundation's supervision.

For the next five years virtually the entire Foundation board was involved with this major restoration project while still performing all of its regular functions and activities. The one board member who undoubtedly contributed most to the success of this ambitious undertaking was Donna Quasthoff, a professional architect who—despite her full-time career—prepared all the plans and specifications for the exterior restoration, handled the various grant funding requirements, and closely supervised the entire project to its successful completion.

The degree of success enjoyed by this project can be measured in part by noting that it earned for the Foundation in February 1979 the Old Santa Fe Association's Award of Merit, and two months later an Award of Honor from the New Mexico Cultural Properties Review Committee.

Apparently, in some cases, it is true that success begets success. By the end of 1979 the Foundation had acquired—mostly through outright gifts and some negotiating—all of the stock in the private El Zaguán, Inc. making that land and building entirely the property of the Foundation. Then in January 1980, about two weeks later, Mr. and Mrs. John Gaw Meem made an outright gift to the Foundation of the Delgado Building, which they had previously purchased and restored. Thus, by the beginning of its twentieth year, the Foundation was the owner of three very valuable and historically important buildings in Santa Fe.

Now, approximately two years later, the heady pleasures of recognition and achievement have been somewhat tempered by the growing awareness of the great responsibilities, decisions, and commitments in time, money, and effort that ownership of these properties entails. This is especially true because these responsibilities and commitments are being superimposed on an already existing ambitious program of activities and obligations, including the almost daily growing demands of new problems and challenges that cannot be ignored. The full impact of this situation is best appreciated with the awareness that virtually the entire program is being handled by one part-time paid executive secretary and a fifteen-person volunteer board, most of whom have full-time occupations and other volunteer commitments.

As a result of these circumstances, the Foundation board will soon have to address the question of whether or not the overall purpose of the Foundation and, indeed, of historic preservation itself, can best be served by continuing to own and maintain all three properties. The alternative would be to relinquish one or more of them to private individuals who have demonstrated the interest, willingness, and ability to accomplish the goals of historic preservation.

The problems and challenges that the Foundation continues to face are exacerbated by increasing economic and social pressures that physically threaten not only the historic fabric of the city, but also the very ordinances that were meant to protect it. These threats usually take the form of attempts to raze or to alter a historic house or building substantially for a more commercial use of the property even when it lies within the designated historic zone. Thus far, the Foundation, acting in some cases on its own and in others with like-minded preservation groups, has been very successful in combating these threats.

The Foundation has learned well that the price of historic preservation is hard work and eternal vigilance.

M. R. (Jim) Adler
February 1982

# Note to the Fourth Edition

The third edition of *Old Santa Fe Today* included, as does this edition, a reprinting of the 1972 preface written by John Gaw Meem as a part of his continuing support of The Historic Santa Fe Foundation. He and his wife, Faith Bemis Meem, played a major role in its founding.

Now, an era has ended. Both John and Faith Meem have departed. They have left the preservation of Santa Fe to those who continue to cherish its historic structures as reminders of its rich cultural heritage. This fourth edition of *Old Santa Fe Today* presents a contemporary view of these historic buildings as they continue to survive in an increasingly urbanized environment.

Since the publication of the third edition in 1982, an additional twelve properties have been awarded the Foundation's **WORTHY OF PRESERVATION** plaque and are included in this edition. They are: Las Acequias, Gustave Baumann House, Edwin Brooks House, Catron Block, Bronson M. Cutting House, Fairview Cemetery, García-Stevenson House, Gross, Kelly and Company Warehouse, Powder House, Archbishop Lamy's Chapel, Salmon-Greer House, and Professor J. A. Wood House. Unfortunately, as noted elsewhere, a few properties previously designated as worthy of preservation have been altered so much that they no longer meet the rigorous standards of the Foundation. The plaques, therefore, have been removed.

In 1988 the untimely death of Marjorie Allen presented the Foundation with the opportunity, and obligation, to acquire and preserve the Roque Tudesqui House, which is situated on East de Vargas Street. This was accomplished with a down payment from existing funds plus assumption of a substantial debt. This acquisition brings the number of Foundation-owned properties to four, including: Pinckney R. Tully House, Felipe R. Delgado House, and El Zaguán. The buildings are not museums. Rather, they are used by people who go about daily activities much as they have since the structures were built. Today, however, those activities must be compatible with the buildings' preservation as authentic historic structures. All the buildings are currently leased for commercial uses such as apartments, offices, and galleries. El Zaguán houses the Foundation office and several apartments and is the site of Bandelier Garden.

An Emergency Acquisition Fund has been established to help preserve historically important structures that might otherwise suffer the fate of the Nusbaum House (see frontispiece). The Foundation's management contract for the Loretto Chapel expired on June 30, 1987. The Chapel remains open to the public during hours specified by the owner.

There has also been a continuing expansion of efforts to inform and educate the public concerning the need, and the techniques required, for historic preservation. These aims are furthered through continuing publication of *The Bulletin*, annual assistance with the publication and distribution of the *Preservation New Mexico* newsletter, tours of historic buildings, and education of younger children with the booklet *We're So Lucky to Live in Santa Fe*, which is distributed to fourth-grade students in the city. Funding also continues for the annual Traditional Christmas Lighting Contest.

Grants have been made for the preservation and restoration of such historic buildings as Cristo Rey Catholic Church, the Meem Auditorium at the Laboratory of Anthropology, and the main entrance doors at the Palace of the Governors History Library (the former Santa Fe Public Library building). Grants have also been designated for Rosario Chapel, Pigeon Ranch, Olive Rush Studio, Randall Davey House, restoration of the Loretto Chapel harmonium, and assistance with other restoration projects.

As always, the price of historic preservation, like that of liberty, continues to be eternal vigilance.

Stephen E. Watkins
November 1990

# Santa Fe's Indigenous Architecture

A brief account of the origin and development of Santa Fe's distinctive architectural styles may help the reader who is unfamiliar with this region to a greater enjoyment of this book. There are two principal regionally historic styles: the Spanish Pueblo and the Territorial.

The Spanish Pueblo, as the name implies, is a style derived from the mixture of Spanish architecture brought in by the Spanish colonizers and that of the Pueblo Indians of the Rio Grande Valley in which Santa Fe is located. The Pueblos, long before Columbus discovered America, had developed traditional forms and techniques of construction admirably suited to this arid country. It is not surprising therefore that the Spaniards, who also came from an arid land, should have adopted the essence of the Indian construction.

This consisted of a unit or room that the Indians combined in many ways to form pueblos, or apartment houses, for communal living and mutual defense. This unit was an approximately rectangular room with stone or puddled adobe walls, an earth floor, and a flat roof. The roof was supported by pine logs, or *vigas,* cut in the nearby forests and laid on top of the walls, about thirty inches apart. These in turn were covered with small poles or *latillas* close to each other at right angles or diagonal to the *vigas.* Next came a bed of brush or weeds on which earth was tamped and graded to drain the water into wooden spouts or *canales* in the parapets that surmounted the walls.

The Spanish colonialists in northern New Mexico, being few in number and far from the centers of Spanish life in Mexico, adopted the basic materials and forms of architecture of the Pueblo Indians. To these they added the technique of shaping adobe into sun-dried bricks, a preference for building on a rough stone foundation rather than directly on the ground, the interior chimneyed fireplace, which was usually placed in a corner, and the *portal.* The flat roof, then, coming down from time immemorial, is the principal characteristic of the Spanish Pueblo style. To this must be added the preponderance of unbroken wall surfaces in relation to door and window openings. This was due to the need to conserve heat in the winter and to keep it out in the summer, and also for defense against enemies.

A complete account of this style, for which space is not available here, would take into account the variations in plan brought from Spain. One of the most prevalent is the house built around an inner *patio,* surrounded with *portales,* or porches, similar to the way Indian pueblo dwellings surround a large central plaza. Santa Fe was full of such houses in the nineteenth century, including those still to be found in the ARIAS DE QUIROS site. Greater detail would also be needed to describe the monumental flat-roofed missions built by the Franciscan friars who came here with the soldiers and colonists. These stone or adobe churches were built with the help of Indian labor, but their techniques were supplemented by Spanish tools and know-how. With these, they shaped logs into richly carved ceiling beams and fashioned elaborate capitals and bolsters, which trace their origin to Moorish Spain, as well as ornamental grilles and doors. Some of these items found their way into civic and domestic architecture. But in general, the exterior of an average house in the Spanish Pueblo style was of adobe, rectangular, with a flat roof surrounded by a low parapet, and soft in outline owing to hand construction and erosion; there were few doors and windows in relation to the wall surfaces.

Santa Fe still has hundreds of such houses—modified through the intervening years—that, while not important enough to be designated as significant or historic buildings, contribute to the overall character of the city. They constitute the main ingredient of Santa Fe's "collective facade."

With the opening of the Santa Fe Trail and the occupation by the American army in 1846, a new style developed, based on the ancient flat-roofed forms of the Spanish Pueblo but strongly modified by new techniques and new materials brought over the trail. Because its development coincided roughly with the period during which New Mexico was a territory, it has been called the Territorial style. Hard-burned brick was brought into the area for the first time but remained expensive and was generally used sparingly in the early Territorial years. Almost the first use to which it was put was to protect the exposed adobe parapets (adobe gradually dissolves and crumbles when exposed to rain and wind) by covering the tops with a few layers of brick, often in decorative patterns. This has become the symbol of the Santa Fe Territorial style and recalls the continuity with the ancient forms based on the flat roof.

The old handmade windows were replaced with mill-made ones with double hung sash. Millwork was brought in to trim the doors and windows that reflected the current Greek Revival styles in St. Louis and Kansas, and was copied locally in a naive and attractive manner. The round posts around the patios and across the facades, with their carved bolster capitals, or corbels, were replaced with slender rectangular columns. Much of the new woodwork was painted white.

Perhaps the most drastic innovation was the covering of the walls with lime and, much later, with cement stucco to protect them against erosion. In the old days the maintenance of adobe plaster was done by women, but with changing customs this was no longer the case, and it became too expensive to hire help for this purpose. While the stucco has introduced a harder line and texture than the soft outline of adobe, it has nevertheless proved to be important; without it many old buildings might not have survived.

The arrival of the railroad in 1880 greatly accelerated the pace of change. Suddenly, a wide range of manufactured building materials were available and self-styled progressive elements of the community pressed to "Americanize" Santa Fe's architecture. Red brick became the favored material for new construction. The old adobe business blocks around the PLAZA gave way to buildings of brick or stone with Italianate facades, of which the best remaining example is the CATRON BLOCK. Nevertheless, in the older neighborhoods the tradition of self-built adobe construction continued undeterred by imported attitudes but builders freely accepted such practical improvements as the metal-sheathed gable roof.

Shortly after the turn of the century, a group of artists and archaeologists, attracted to the area by its pre-American cultures, began a movement to reverse the trend toward Americanization and return Santa Fe to her architectural roots. Taking up the task of defining an authentic, "indigenous" architecture of the region, they sought to convince the business community of the suitability as well as the economic advantage of retaining, restoring, and recreating a distinctly local style for both commercial and domestic uses. From these efforts evolved the Spanish Pueblo Revival and Territorial Revival styles.

There is still a third classification possible for Santa Fe buildings, which reflects the styles of the outside world rather than local regional conditions. Typical are the ST. FRANCIS CATHEDRAL and the UNITED STATES COURT HOUSE. To preserve Santa Fe's unique Pueblo-Territorial heritage, however, the city's Historic Zoning Ordinance, first enacted in 1957, now prohibits buildings designed in other styles from being erected within the historic area.

Barn of *jacal* construction (JUAN JOSÉ PRADA HOUSE, text on p. 84).
*Karl Kernberger, photographer*

# Plaquing Santa Fe Historic Property

The plaquing of buildings that have been found to be of historic importance is central to the Foundation's mission of increasing public awareness of Santa Fe's heritage. Bronze plaques reading "The Historic Santa Fe Foundation Finds This Building Worthy of Preservation" have been placed on more than fifty buildings in Santa Fe and its environs.

All structures chosen for this recognition must meet the following criterion:

- they must retain their historic character, that is, they must not have been so altered that they no longer convey their historic associations.

They must also meet at least one of three further criteria:

- they must embody the distinguishing characteristics of an architecture identified with the history of Santa Fe
- be the site of significant events in that history
- be associated with the lives of persons prominent in that history.

Buildings of recent historical importance and those constructed within the past fifty years are rarely considered.

Requests for plaquing are handled by the Foundation's research committee. Usually at the request of a property owner, members of the committee evaluate the building's present condition to determine whether it still has historic and architectural integrity. The committee then seeks to document the historical significance of the building and presents the results of this research to the full board for its vote. The documentation on newly plaqued buildings is published in the Foundation's *Bulletin* and is included in future editions of its publication, *Old Santa Fe Today*. Most of these properties have also been placed on the State Register of Cultural Properties and several are on the National Register of Historic Places.

The Historic Santa Fe Foundation is totally independent of any governmental entity or agency and recognition by it places no legal restrictions upon an owner as to what may be done with the plaqued property in the future. The Foundation asks owners to sign a simple agreement that states that if the building is significantly altered, the plaque will be returned at the Foundation's request.

Unfortunately, this has become necessary in three cases. In each instance, the reasons for unplaquing have been such serious alterations that the house no longer projected its original characteristics.

El Rancho Viejo in Tesuque appeared only in the second edition of *Old Santa Fe Today*. During the 1830s, it was a portion of the large country estate of Juan Bautista Vigil y Alaríd, an important *rico* and politician during the brief period when New Mexico was part of the Mexican Republic.

The Roque Lobato House was recognized in the first and second editions as one of the oldest structures on record in Santa Fe. It was built soon after 1785 by Roque Lobato, armorer and soldier of the Spanish royal garrison of Santa Fe, on land granted him by Governor Juan Bautista de Anza.

The third house to be unplaqued, the Juan Rodríguez House, had been in all three previous editions. However, it was stated that "very little of this house can be seen today, but the older part is of architectural interest because of its nineteenth-century New Mexican detail." The researcher concluded by saying, "Most of the present structures on the Juan Rodriguez property were remodeled or built in 1969–70." This work has continued so that today it no longer bears any resemblance to an earlier period.

It is this attention to our mission that has helped preserve the sympathetic feeling that so many people continue to have for Santa Fe.

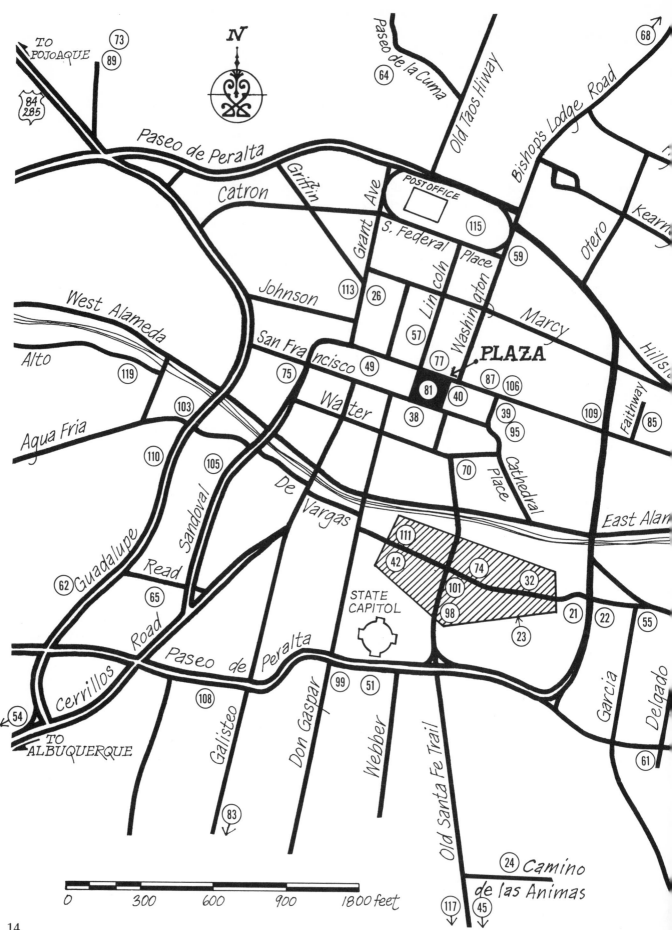

14

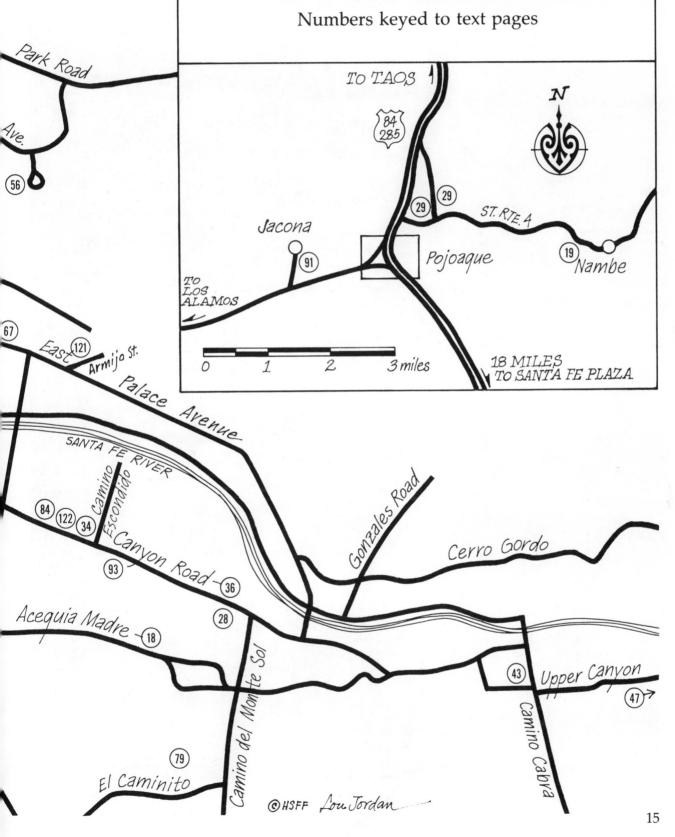

# MAP OF PLAQUED HISTORIC BUILDINGS

Numbers keyed to text pages

Park Road

Ave.

(56)

To TAOS

84 285

N

(29) (29)

ST. RTE. A

Jacona

(91)

Pojoaque

(19) Nambe

TO LOS ALAMOS

0   1   2   3 miles

18 MILES TO SANTA FE PLAZA

(67)

East

(121) Armijo St.

Palace Avenue

SANTA FE RIVER

Camino Escondido

(84) (122) (34)

(93)

Canyon Road

(36)

Gonzales Road

Cerro Gordo

Acequia Madre (18)

(28)

Camino del Monte Sol

(43) Upper Canyon

(47)

Camino Cabra

(79)

El Caminito

© HSFF  Lou Jordan

15

# La Villa de Santa Fe

In the winter of 1609–10, ten years before the Pilgrims landed at Plymouth Rock, the Villa of Santa Fe was founded as the seat of government for the vast region of the Southwest, then under the rule of the viceroy of New Spain (Mexico). It has been the capital of New Mexico since that date, and is therefore the oldest capital city in the United States. Santa Fe still retains much of its original Spanish character.

Seventy years earlier, the northern Mexican frontier, including Arizona and New Mexico, had been explored by Francisco Vásquez de Coronado, the young governor of the province of Nueva Vizcaya. In 1598 the first Spanish settlement in this region was established by Don Juan de Oñate on the east side of the Rio Grande near San Juan Pueblo; it was relocated across the river in 1599. The colony was moved to the site of Santa Fe in 1610 by Governor Pedro de Peralta, acting under orders from the viceroy to found a new capital.

There is archaeological evidence that portions of Santa Fe were built on the site of an early Indian pueblo known as *Kuapoge,* or "place of shell beads near the water," but this prehistoric ruin was obliterated by the time the Spaniards arrived.

Throughout the 200 years of Spanish rule that followed its establishment, the walled city of Santa Fe was headquarters for political administration as well as for further exploration and missionary work among the Indians. Its only supply line was the *Camino Real,* royal road, stretching hundreds of miles south by caravan and horseback to Chihuahua and Mexico City, through arid, hostile country. Until the successful revolt of Mexico from Spain in 1821, foreign explorers and traders were not welcome in the province of Nuevo Méjico, and in 1807, Lieutenant Zebulon Pike, for whom Pike's Peak was named, was brought here as a prisoner for trespassing on Spanish soil.

Within a few months of Mexican independence, however, William Becknell of Missouri was met by New Mexican troops south of the Raton Pass and encouraged to come to Santa Fe with the first load of U.S. trade goods, thereby opening the famous Santa Fe Trail. From that time until after occupation by the United States, the city served as the vital link between traders from the east and from Mexico.

At the beginning of war between Mexico and this country, the Department of New Mexico was annexed to the United States. On August 18, 1846, Brigadier General Stephen Watts Kearny, commander of the Army of the West, marched his troops into Santa Fe and raised the U.S. flag over the PALACE OF THE GOVERNORS. In anticipation of trouble that never came, FORT MARCY was built on a hill northeast of the city, where its ruins remain as a symbol of America's Manifest Destiny of westward expansion to the Pacific.

View of the PLAZA with the obelisk, center, and the CATRON BLOCK, background, right.
*Bart Durham, photographer*

# Acequia Madre

The old *acequias*, or irrigation ditches, of Santa Fe are almost things of the past, but the Acequia Madre, Mother Ditch, still flows along the street that bears its name and reminds us of what was once a vital part of the city's existence.

In the southeast section of Santa Fe, this *acequia* is still important to many persons who use its water to irrigate their fruit trees and grazing lands.

Ditch irrigation had long been used in the arid regions of Spain, as well as by Indians of the Southwest. When the Spanish colonists came, they brought both the engineering knowledge and a body of irrigation law necessary to build and regulate water systems throughout the province of New Mexico. For more than 300 years these *acequia* systems have operated effectively. In rural areas and many towns they are still maintained and cherished.

Shortly after the founding of Santa Fe, both the *acequia madre* on the south side of town and the *acequia de la muralla* skirting the low hills on the north were built to provide water for irrigation and the domestic needs of the community. In the Urrutia map of the 1760s, the line of the northern *acequia* may be traced along the early wall, or *muralla*, which

helped fortify the city, at the approximate location of present Hillside Avenue. In the early Spanish period, water for the PALACE OF THE GOVERNORS came from two *acequias* that apparently ran from the *cienega*, or springs, to the east. One flowed down present Palace Avenue in front of the building; the other watered gardens in the rear. By cutting off the water from these *acequias*, the Indians forced the Spaniards to evacuate in the Pueblo Revolt and by the same method, de Vargas drove the Indians out of the Palace in 1693. Later other *acequias* carried water to the ecclesiastical lands and adjoining property in the city.

Few recognizable traces of these *acequias* remain, but the Acequia Madre has never ceased to flow, and it is still governed by the old Spanish laws, with a *mayordomo de la acequia* and three commissioners to supervise its upkeep. An annual fee is paid by all property owners along the ditch who still hold water rights, and it is their duty to help clean out the *acequia* in the spring, as well as to assist when further help is needed during the irrigation season.

The ditch on Acequia Madre Street, with the water running.
*Tony Perry, photographer*

A water diversion gate, one of a series still in use along the six-mile length of the ACEQUIA MADRE.
*Vincent Foster, photographer*

LAS ACEQUIAS, Spanish Pueblo Revival estate on the Nambé River.
*Agnesa Reeve, photographer*

# Las Acequias

## (Cyrus McCormick, Jr. House)
## Nambé, New Mexico (private residence)

One of the most striking examples of the Spanish Pueblo Revival is Las Acequias, the 1931 adobe house architect John Gaw Meem built in Nambé for Cyrus McCormick, Jr. The house, which was three years in the planning and construction, is situated about fifteen miles north of Santa Fe near the Nambé River and surrounded by lush meadows and towering old cottonwoods. Its design was the result of a collaboration between Meem and artist-archaeologist Carlos Vierra, two of the best qualified proponents of the Spanish Pueblo Revival style.

McCormick, of the McCormick Harvester family, bought his Nambé land almost 200 years after Don Gaspar Domingo de Mendoza, Governor and Captain General of the Kingdom, had granted it to Vicente Duran de Armijo in 1739. Armijo, "resident

of the town of Santa Fe, a settler and conqueror of this Kingdom of New Mexico," had, according to his petition, "experienced innumerable sufferings and hunger and nakedness and other misfortunes" while carrying out his obligations as a loyal subject of Spain.

During 1929 and 1930 McCormick collected 100 acres of the grant in small parcels and instituted a series of letters and conferences with Meem and Vierra, which would culminate in a unique structure.

The arrangement of rooms finally agreed upon is linear in the Spanish tradition. However, three wings are joined in roughly the shape of a Y with the main entrance at its apex, a service wing to the right, and living and bedroom wings projecting left and forward. Tucked into the west brow of a hill, and including many *portales*, the residence is oriented for spectacular views rather than protection from the weather.

Its situation and 180-foot-long facade give the house an extraordinarily low silhouette. The pink-brown adobe has four or five levels of long, low horizontals forming a roofline that, from its entrance court, appears to rise above the ground less than a full story.

Exterior details, such as battered walls and sloping parapets, adobe plaster, wooden *canales,* and deeply inset windows and doors with heavy wood lintels and sills, reflect New Mexican architecture as it was until 1821 and the opening of the Santa Fe Trail. This residence is one of the few remaining examples of mud-plastered exterior walls.

Interiors echo traditional design, and in some cases incorporate elements retrieved from old structures. For example, a board in the dining room ceiling bears the inscription. *"En el año de 1895 el día 20 de julio se techo este cuarto el carpentero* [sic] *Salvío de Martínez."*

Gracefully, Las Acequias reflects the Spanish Pueblo Revival style at its most lavish.

Entry *zaguán* with San José Mission doors, LAS ACEQUIAS.
*Agnesa Reeve, photographer*

20

ALARÍD HOUSE, with the pitched tin roof more common to northern New Mexico villages than to Santa Fe. Courtesy of Cultural Properties Review Committee, Historic Preservation Division, State of New Mexico.
*Karl Kernberger, photographer*

# José Alaríd House

**338 East de Vargas Street**

On December 20, 1835, José Alaríd, a disabled Mexican Army veteran of the Santa Fe Presidial Company, purchased a tract of farmland from Sergeant Francisco Campos. On this property the José Alaríd House, sometimes referred to as "The House of Sixty-one Vigas," was constructed and during its history was owned by several prominent Santa Fe residents.

The property was sold to Joseph Hersch in 1854 and was in turn sold to Bishop Jean Baptiste Lamy on February 26, 1859; what use he made of the house is not known. Five years later Bishop Lamy transferred ownership of the property to Epifanio Vigil, son of Donaciano Vigil, both of whom were active in public affairs. Among other positions he held, Donaciano was acting civil governor of New Mexico. Epifanio served as territorial auditor from 1865 to 1869 and was appointed official interpreter by the governor in 1868.

In 1911 the property was conveyed to Anita J. Chapman, the eldest child of James L. and Jesusita Johnson, owners of EL ZAGUÁN in the mid-1800s. Chapman worked as translator and secretary for Adolf F. Bandelier, a renowned anthropologist who became a close friend of the family. She also served as territorial librarian—the first woman to hold that position—and as state librarian from 1917 to 1937.

BANDELIER HOUSE, west *portal.*
*Karl Kernberger, photographer*

# Adolph Bandelier House

**352 East de Vargas Street (private residence)**

The most famous occupant of this large adobe house was Adolph Francis Bandelier, pioneer archaeologist and ethnohistorian who made it his home while conducting research in New Mexico, Arizona, and Mexico during 1882–92.

The building is Territorial in style and has been extensively enlarged and remodeled without, however, losing its integrity. The first deed of record is the sale of the property to Marta Romero y Maynas, February 1, 1867, in which the house was described as having "three and one-half portals," of which only the one on the west still remains. The front entrance then faced south. In 1873 it was bought by John F. Schumann, who rented it to Bandelier.

Born in Berne, Switzerland, in 1840, Bandelier made his first trip to New Mexico in 1880. After a year of archaeological investigation in Mexico and Central America, he returned to Santa Fe and spent much of the next ten years conducting his research

in the region. He was the first scholar to attempt a comprehensive, scientific study of the archaeology, ethnography, and historical documentation of the New Mexico Indians. He traveled thousands of miles on foot and horseback and often lived for weeks at a time in Indian villages.

He was author of *The Delight Makers,* a novel of prehistoric Pueblo Indians, major scientific works, and articles on anthropological and historical subjects.

On February 11, 1914, shortly before Bandelier's death in Seville, Spain, President Woodrow Wilson proclaimed the ruins of Indian cliff dwellers in Frijoles Canyon the Bandelier National Monument.

In December 1919 the house was bought by Santa Fe merchant Henry S. Kaune, whose wife was Elise C. Bandelier, a niece of the famous anthropologist. They made extensive additions to the house.

BARRIO DE ANALCO plaque located near the corner of East de Vargas and Old Santa Fe Trail.
*Vincent Foster, photographer*

*Portal*-covered section of the BARRIO DE ANALCO on Old Santa Fe Trail (formerly College Street).
*Tony Perry, photographer*

# Barrio de Analco

This *barrio*, or district, in the center of which is the CHAPEL OF SAN MIGUEL, is the oldest settlement of European origin in Santa Fe except for the PLAZA, and hence one of the oldest in the United States. Originally settled in the 1600s by Tlaxcalan Indian servants from Mexico who came with the Franciscan missionaries and Spanish officials, it took the Nahuatl word *analco* (the other side of the water) to distinguish it from the PLAZA area, which was on the north side of the Rio de Santa Fe. Soon after the Barrio de Analco was settled, the original CHAPEL OF SAN MIGUEL was built to serve as the mission church.

During the Pueblo Revolt of 1680, the Barrio de Analco was the first section of Santa Fe to be sacked and razed by attackers from "all the Tanos and Pecos nations, and the Querez of San Marcos armed and giving war-whoops." The rebels approached through the cultivated fields to the south. Those residents who escaped took refuge in the PALACE OF THE GOVERNORS with the beleaguered Spaniards and later retreated with Governor Otermín to El Paso. After the reconquest only a few of its former settlers returned, but the Barrio was soon rebuilt by others.

By 1776 the Barrio de Analco was occupied by married soldiers, *genízaro* servants (Indians living in a Europeanized status), and other laborers. It is probable that some buildings still standing in this area were built before that date.

Several buildings described on the following pages are located within the Barrio de Analco. This concentration of structures, deemed worthy of preservation from both historical and architectural standpoints, provides an authentic setting for the CHAPEL OF SAN MIGUEL and points up the significance and importance of the Barrio to Santa Fe.

BAUMANN HOUSE, with porch posts carved by the artist, and original gate and fencing.
*Vincent Foster, photographer*

# Gustave Baumann House

### 409 Camino de las Animas (private residence)

The house was built by Gustave Bauman in 1923 on three lots bought in that same year from Walter L. Miller. In 1914 Miller had platted a small addition on the north side of what was then called East Buena Vista Street. An internationally known artist and prominent member of Santa Fe's art colony, Baumann designed the house and crafted its highly personal interior decor.

Born in 1881 in Magdeburg, Germany, Baumann immigrated with his family to Chicago at the age of ten. By the time he was sixteen he was studying at The Art Institute of Chicago and had begun working in commercial art. In 1905 he returned to Munich, then a popular place for young artists, to study and spent a year at the Königliche Kunstgewerbenschule. The Art Institute of Chicago honored him in 1905 with an exhibit of his wood carvings that featured an entire toy village. After several years in Brown County, Indiana, Baumann came to New Mexico and remained in Santa Fe until his death in 1971.

Baumann was one of the foremost color print makers of his time and one of the first non-Oriental artists to create multicolored works, each made from a series of precisely carved wood blocks. His style was realistic and his strong interest in Southwest Indian art and native themes is frequently evident in his work. In 1939 he published a book, *Frijoles Canyon Pictographs,* of twenty-six wood-cut representations of pictographs from caves in Frijoles Canyon. This book was selected as one of the "Fifty Books of the Year."

The house was designed by Baumann and translated into formal plans by architect Charles Gaastra. It was built around a windowless interior room which had steel doors and served as a fireproof storage room for wood blocks, prints, and valuable papers.

The unassuming exterior belies the eccentricity of the interior. Although built of adobe, the design is not a strong expression of a traditional adobe style. The main facade is organized symmetrically with a slightly higher center section and two recessed side wings. Detailing on the exterior carved by Baumann includes two porch posts. On the roof is a wrought iron figure he designed from the letters in the word "koshare," a Pueblo dance character. He used this as a logo and it appears on a number of his oils in place of a signature. The wooden gates and low fence enclosing a small front yard are original.

The unique qualities of the interior are encountered immediately. The entrance leads directly into a long octagonal room lit by a large octagonal skylight. The eight sides of this room were created by adding a plane at each of the four corners and giving each a function—radiators in the southeast and southwest corners, a door on the northeast, and a fireplace on the northwest. The walls of this room, and much of the rest of the house, are painted a dark mustard yellow with a mottled effect that was created by Baumann with a sponge. There are Indian-derived designs painted along the top of the walls in green, red, white, and black. Called the "little gallery" by Jane Baumann, this room was used to receive guests and as a gallery where prints were shown and sold.

On the west side of the house the small dining room is decorated with shelves and a cupboard designed and built by Baumann. There is also an original ceiling fixture. Baumann always came in from his studio at tea time and friends often visited then.

About 1932 Baumann began carving marionettes and eventually created a marionette theater. The entire collection, including the theater, sets, and nearly seventy marionettes, is now a part of the collection of New Mexico's Museum of Fine Arts. Ceiling hooks that held rolled canvas backdrops are the only reminders of the marionette theater in the house today.

Other more readily visible achievements are Baumann's contributions to two of Santa Fe's churches. In the 1930s he restored *La Conquistadora* for the Archdiocese and also carved a replica. In the mid-1940s he spent two years carving a *reredos* for the Episcopal Church of the Holy Faith.

Entrance gallery radiator screen made from Baumann wood blocks.
*Vincent Foster, photographer*

BERGERE HOUSE, originally Fort Marcy officer's quarters.
*Bart Durham, photographer*

# A. M. Bergere House

### 135 Grant Avenue

The A. M. Bergere House was built in the early 1870s as an officer's quarters on the Fort Marcy Military Reservation, created by President Andrew Johnson's Executive Order of August 28, 1868. Quarters for the commanding officers were established north of the PALACE OF THE GOVERNORS and fronting Washington Avenue. Six other adobe houses for officers of lesser rank and their families were also constructed, symmetrically positioned so that half the houses faced Lincoln Avenue and the other half faced Grant Avenue. Of these six structures, only the Bergere House at the northwest corner and the FORT MARCY OFFICER'S RESIDENCE at the southeast corner have survived.

The army abandoned the Fort Marcy Military Reservation on October 10, 1894, and the post was placed under the custody of the Interior Department for disposal. Until this could be accomplished, the property was to be administered by the governor of New Mexico. During this period, the six officers' quarters were used as rent-free residences by politicians and prominent New Mexicans.

On June 3, 1899, Solomon Luna was granted permission to occupy the Bergere House. The Lunas, Oteros, and Chaveses were the three most influential and politically powerful families of the Rio Abajo (Lower River) region during the Mexican and Territorial periods. In addition to Solomon, the Luna family also included Tranquilino, Jesús, María, Luz, and Eloisa, who married Manuel B. Otero in 1879.

Three years after the death of her husband, Eloisa Luna Otero married Alfred Maurice Bergere. Of Italian ancestry, Bergere immigrated to the United States from England in 1872 and six years later moved to Valencia County where he was involved in mercantile, stock-raising, and insurance interests. On February 28, 1901, the secretary of the interior authorized Governor Miguel A. Otero to permit Bergere, then district court clerk of the first judicial district, to occupy a building on the Fort Marcy Abandoned Military Reservation as soon as one became available. In a letter dated May 4 of the same year, Governor Otero informed the Department of the Interior that no houses were vacant but that A. M. Bergere was occupying the house assigned to his brother-in-law, Solomon Luna.

On January 5, 1904, the Fort Marcy Abandoned Military Reservation was conveyed to the City of Santa Fe, which in turn transferred the property to the Santa Fe board of education. Mrs. Otero purchased the house and the two lots from the board of education on December 22, 1905, for $2,700.

Originally, the A. M. Bergere House was L-shaped, with a cross-gabled roof of pleated "tin" crowned with three fired brick chimneys. The exterior walls were mud-plastered and the two front corners were rectangularly etched to simulate dressed stone corner trim. Over the years the exterior of the house has been altered. In 1926 the cross-gabled roof on the main portion of the house was removed: the upper story was squared and a flat roof added to make the structure conform to the Spanish Pueblo style of architecture that was experiencing a revival in the capital city at that time. The stables and tennis court constructed by Bergere no longer exist, but the trees he planted are still bearing fruit.

# Rafael Borrego House

**724 Canyon Road**

The Territorial-style BORREGO HOUSE.
*Len Bouché, photographer*

Early records for many houses in this area have not been found. There is, however, a Spanish deed for the property in which the Borrego House is located dated September 14, 1753, at which time it was sold to Gerónimo López by Ysidro Martín, a soldier in the Spanish army who may originally have received it as a grant for military service. The conveyance was for farmland described as bounded on the south by the ACEQUIA MADRE and on the north by "a Royal Road which comes down from the mountain range," now known as CANYON ROAD.

In his will dated 1769, Gerónimo López stated that he owned two houses, one newly built, adjoining an orchard of fourteen trees and farmland. His widow later sold the property to Gerónimo Gonzáles, and because she was unable to write her name, Gonzáles, as buyer, witnessed the deed for her. In 1839 he in turn sold it to his son-in-law, Rafael Borrego, and for more than seventy-five years thereafter it was owned by members of the Borrego family.

During the late nineteenth century the Borregos added the large front room, and as they were prominent in New Mexico political circles, it was probably the scene of many political gatherings and social events. The long front *portal* with tapered, hand-hewn columns, windows, and doors, typical of the territorial period, may have been added at the same time.

When Rafael Borrego died, sometime between 1839 and 1845, half of the property was inherited by his children and the other half by his widow, María Refugio Gonzáles de Borrego. When she died in 1872, she left her residence—a three-room house with a hall and *portal*—to her son, Pablo. A room *abajo*, below, was willed to a servant. It was a common practice in those days to bequeath individual rooms, and sometimes parts of rooms, to one's children as their inheritance, thereby creating many deed complications for later generations to untangle. It was not until 1939 that all portions of the house came again into a single ownership.

By 1906 the property had passed out of Borrego hands, and after a series of different owners the main portion of the house was bought for preservation in 1928 by Margretta S. Dietrich, who had acquired EL ZAGUÁN for the same purpose the previous year. In 1939 she bought the remaining two rooms and had the house restored under the supervision of Mrs. Kenneth L. Chapman. In 1931 the house received the Cyrus McCormick prize for the best restoration of a residence during the preceding two years. In 1940 the house was selected for study by the Historic American Buildings Survey, and drawings of its plans are now on file in the Library of Congress.

After later ownerships, when the future of the famous old house seemed endangered, it was bought by the Old Santa Fe Association. They subsequently resold the building with restrictive covenants to insure its continued preservation.

View under the *portal*, BOUQUET RANCH. Note *zaguán* entrance with two preservation plaques.
*Vincent Foster, photographer*

# Bouquet Ranch

**Pojoaque, New Mexico (private residence)**

# Jail House Ranch

**Pojoaque, New Mexico (private residence)**

The land and sprawling collection of buildings near the Indian pueblo of Pojoaque known as "Bouquet Ranch" and "Jail House Ranch" were part of the country estate of Nicolás Ortiz III and his second wife, Josefa Bustamante. Ortiz was killed by Comanches in 1769. Their property extended for some two miles along the north bank of the Nambé River, ending on the west at the present road from Santa Fe to Taos. The properties exemplify the Spanish adaptation of the native Indian building traditions. Each unit is constructed of adobe brick, and ceilings are spanned by *vigas* overlayed by wood decking.

29

Initially, the roofs were dirt. In the original buildings, rooms open into interior courtyards; exterior walls face the treelined roadside.

Nicolás's son, Antonio José, inherited the western part, now known as the Bouquet Ranch, then secured the portion received by his stepmother, who was also his sister-in-law, for "satisfaction of debt," and purchased additional land on both sides of the river. During the same period, he also enlarged the NICOLÁS ORTIZ III HOUSE on San Francisco Street to include the portion that bears his name.

When Antonio José made his will, he divided the lands and "El Rancho de Pujuaque [sic] with its two big houses and other small houses in which the servants live," according to the usual Spanish legal custom, among his wife, children, and grandchildren whose fathers had died. In her will of 1814,

the widow, Rosa Bustamante, made a further partition of her portion. The greater portion of the Pojoaque property, as well as the Santa Fe residence, however, came into the hands of the eldest son, Antonio de Jesús who, in turn, fragmented it among his many heirs by his will of 1837. During the next thirty years, the holdings north of the Nambé River and for a mile east of the Taos road were split up into many small parcels owned by relatives or servants of the Ortiz family.

In 1867 Jean (who, in later years, also signed his name John and Juan) Bouquet, a Frenchman who had operated a store and wine shop in Santa Fe for several years, began buying land north of the Rio Nambé that was previously owned by Nicolás, Antonio José, and Antonio de Jesús Ortiz, as well as parcels west of the Taos road. By the time he died in 1897, Bouquet and his wife, Petra Larragoite, had

JAIL HOUSE RANCH interior.
*Bart Durham, photographer*

JAIL HOUSE RANCH entry.
*Vincent Foster, photographer*

made two land transfers and purchased twenty-two pieces of property that contained four houses and a mill built by Antonio de Jesús Ortiz. Among the sellers were various members of the Ortiz family and several Pojoaque Indians.

Bouquet was famous throughout the region for his horticultural talents. He was one of the first farmers in the valley skilled in the technique of grafting to improve the quality of his produce. His large orchard contained many new varieties of imported fruit trees. He held a government forage contract to furnish hay and grain for the military post in Santa Fe, which he filled from his own excellent crops and those purchased from his neighbors. Bouquet remodeled existing buildings and constructed others to form a sizable complex that included a general store. Bouquet Ranch, including what is now Jail House Ranch, was also a stage stop and a hostelry with a reputation for good food.

When Bouquet died in 1897, his widow inherited the ranch. Two years later she married Cicero Weidner who, in 1907, signed an affidavit renouncing all claims to her property in return for receiving ownership to the eastern, or Jail House Ranch, portion. According to local tradition, the property was used to house convict labor when known as the Alfalfa Farms Company. Bars on some of the windows substantiate this claim.

In 1917 Bouquet Ranch had come into the possession of J. H. and Adele B. Crist, but land deeds are silent as to the means by which the well-known attorney and politician acquired the property except for a statement in a later conveyance that he received it for "twenty years of legal service to the widow, Petra L. de Bouquet de Weidner." The Crists received a U.S. patent to a parcel of land in 1930 as the result of the settlement of the Pojoaque Pueblo Indian land claim by the Pueblo Lands Board. The buildings were significantly remodeled during the Crists' residency.

BOYLE HOUSE.
*Vincent Foster, photographer*

# Arthur Boyle House

### 327 East de Vargas Street (private residence)

This large adobe house east of the BARRIO DE ANALCO has had a long history. It appears on the Urrutia map of 1766–68 as a sizable, hacienda-like building, and also on the Gilmer map of 1846. Who the earliest owners were is unknown, but in the early 1800s, the house and outlying lands constituted the *rancho* of Salvador Martín, who conveyed the property to Antonio de Jesús Ortiz, son of the famous, wealthy landowner, Antonio José Ortiz. In his will of 1837, Antonio de Jesús bequeathed the property to his daughter Ana María, wife of Juan José Romero. She sold it to the Very Reverend Peter Eguillon, vicar general to Bishop Lamy, in 1863, and four years later the church conveyed it to Morris Bloom-field and Colonel Herbert M. Enos of the quarter-master corps.

Bloomfield sold his interest to telegraph operator Joseph Gough and his wife in 1874. Enos and the new owners divided the property along the line of a hall that ran through the house. Shortly thereafter, Enos left New Mexico after providing that his half, on the east, be held in trust for his two minor and illegitimate daughters. The trustee was James L. Johnson, then owner of EL ZAGUÁN. In 1881 the Goughs sold the west portion to Arthur Boyle, son-in-law of and New Mexico representative for English land speculator William Blackmore. The property was again joined in 1889 when the Enos daughters conveyed the east section to Blanche Blackmore Boyle. The Boyles added a northern tier of rooms to what remained of the original structure.

Massive adobe walls, in some places more than four feet thick, and ceilings of *rajas*, or split wood, overlaid with straw and earth, are evidence that the house was built at an early date. Territorial details include typical squared-off ceiling beams, a long rear *portal*, a manteled fireplace, and a bay window at the back of the house.

Corner fireplace with raised hearth, BOYLE HOUSE. *Vincent Foster, photographer*

BOYLE HOUSE interior. Note the *vigas* with cedar *rajas*, the painted wall trim at floor level, and the double-adobe walls. *Tony Perry, photographer*

BROOKS HOUSE entry *placita* with original *portal*.
*Vincent Foster, photographer*

# Edwin Brooks House

**553 Canyon Road (private residence)**
**Fremont Ellis studio open by appointment**

Artist William Penhallow Henderson created this house by remodeling and enlarging an old adobe that had been purchased by his son-in-law, John Evans, in 1923. Shortly after his marriage, Evans, who was the son of Taos's Mabel Dodge Luhan, formed the Flying Heart Development Corporation and purchased this property from James Baca. Baca, the grandson of James L. Johnson, had purchased the property in 1918. Before that it had been owned by the Moya family for many years. James Baca

also owned his grandfather's property, EL ZAGUÁN, which is located immediately west of the Brooks House.

Henderson and his wife, poet Alice Corbin, came to New Mexico from Chicago in 1916. Founding members of Santa Fe's art colony, they were for many years among its guiding spirits. In addition to producing well-received easel paintings and murals, Henderson became an active participant in the movement to revive adobe architecture.

In 1926 Henderson formed the Pueblo Spanish Building Company with Edwin Brooks as a minor shareholder. Among his best-known architectural commissions were the remodeled Sena Plaza and the Wheelwright Museum. In the mid-1920s he also began to design furniture based on Spanish Colonial originals that local artisans hand-built for him.

For the Brooks House, Henderson provided architectural designs and also served as building contractor, using only native workmen and artisans. A second story was added, creating the most striking feature of the interior—the two-story living room and balcony. Throughout the house, there is an abundance of hand-adzed wood used for such elements as large supporting beams, massive exposed lintels, and the staircase to the second floor. Examples of carved wood are found in balustrades and decorative wooden grilles in front of radiators. In addition, each room has built-in furniture made of hand-adzed wood.

Edwin Brooks bought the property in 1928 and lived in the house from 1931 until 1937. Although not an artist himself, he was active in artistic circles, particularly the Little Theatre, as was his wife, Virginia Morley. The subsequent history of the house included several changes of ownership until it was rented and then purchased in 1963 by Fremont Ellis. An early member of the art colony and one of the group of painters known as *Los Cinco Pintores* in the early 1920s, Ellis lived in the house for nearly thirty years until his death in 1985. It remains in the Ellis family today.

BROOKS HOUSE interior detailing, designed by artist William Penhallow Henderson.
*Vincent Foster, photographer*

A view of CANYON ROAD, recording the diversity of structures on this art colony street.
*Vincent Foster, photographer*

# Canyon Road

Canyon Road is the center of Santa Fe's art colony and one of the older districts of the city. Before the Spanish conquest, an Indian trail along the Santa Fe River followed the course of the present street and led over the Sangre de Cristo Mountains to the pueblo of Pecos. Spanish authorities designated the trail as *el camino del cañon*, the road of the canyon. After crossing the mountains, it joined the main road to Pecos on the plain east of town.

The road was used by woodcutters to bring firewood, heavily loaded on the backs of their burros, to customers in the city.

For many years lower Canyon Road was the scene of the annual Corpus Christi procession, which was routed from ST. FRANCIS CATHEDRAL along the Alameda to the old Castillo Street Bridge (since replaced by a wider structure), then up to Canyon Road under flower-trimmed arches to the Delgado Street corner. Here, the archbishop pronounced the benediction before an altar erected for the occasion by the Delgado family.

Beginning at the corner of García Street and extending far up the canyon, the winding, narrow street has succeeded in retaining much of its character, in part because of the number of old adobe structures along its informal street line. Many of these houses are built almost flush with the pavement. They contain residences, shops, art galleries, studios, restaurants, and neighborhood services appropriate to Canyon Road's designation by city ordinance as a "residential arts and crafts zone." The unpaved streets that branch off Canyon Road and ACEQUIA MADRE, irregular, shady, and narrow, look very much as they did in the past.

The old Indian trail over the mountain was reopened in 1900 by rangers from the Pecos River Forest Reserve. In 1932 however, the Public Service Company closed the Santa Fe Canyon to visitors. The road is populated for approximately four miles, as far as the RANDALL DAVEY HOUSE.

Old buildings along winding CANYON ROAD. Note the rubble wall, right, and the structures built directly on the street.
*Laura Gilpin, photographer*

# La Castrense

## 68 East San Francisco Street

One of the finest eighteenth-century New Mexico churches once stood on this site, according to the description of Bishop Tamarón, who visited Santa Fe during its construction in 1760, and the later account of Fr. Francisco Atanasio Domínguez in 1776. This was the chapel of Our Lady of Light, or La Castrense, the military chapel for the presidial company of Santa Fe.

La Castrense was erected at the expense of Governor Francisco Marín del Valle on land he had bought on the south side of the PLAZA. Artisans brought from Mexico by the governor carved the handsome *reredos*, or altar screen, from white stone quarried in the Jacona region north of Santa Fe. Special high masses were occasionally celebrated in La Castrense and *Te Deums* sung to commemorate victories in Indian campaigns. Among prominent persons buried in the chapel were Bernardo Miera y Pacheco and Francisco de Anza, brother of Governor Juan Bautista de Anza, both in 1785.

By 1835 the chapel was closed because the Mexican government no longer provided funds for chaplains. After 1846, when U.S. forces occupied the city, it was used as an ammunition storeroom, then refitted for use by the district court of the first judicial district. In August 1851 former governor Donaciano Vigil protested against such secular use of a consecrated building. After some contention, the court was moved to the PALACE OF THE GOVERNORS, and La Castrense was formally returned to Bishop Jean Baptiste Lamy. For several years it was again used as a place of worship.

In 1859 the bishop sold the east portion of the property to Levi Spiegelberg, and the following year he deeded the building and the remaining land to merchant Simon Delgado in exchange for "$2,000 to make repairs on the parroquia," plus a deed to Delgado's land near SAN MIGUEL CHAPEL, where Bishop Lamy wished to build a boys' school.

When La Castrense was sold in 1859 the carved stone *reredos* was carefully removed to the old *parroquia* and placed in the sanctuary. There it remained concealed by a wall after the present cathedral was built (1869–86). In 1940 it was installed in the new CRISTO REY CATHOLIC CHURCH. Corbels and *vigas*

from La Castrense were also placed in the SANTUARIO DE GUADALUPE on Guadalupe Street.

During partial demolition in 1859, the chapel's north walls were taken down. Shops and warehouses were built as far back as sixty feet from the present sidewalk, covering the small cemetery. Some of the remaining interior walls were still standing as late as 1955. Before they were torn down, the walls were measured and studied during excavation by the Laboratory of Anthropology of the Museum of New Mexico.

LA CASTRENSE commemorative plaque, south side of the PLAZA at 58 East San Francisco Street. *Vincent Foster, photographer*

Entrance to CATHEDRAL PARK, a French-style park with an *allée* of trees that originally led to the entrance of St. Vincent Sanitorium.
*Vincent Foster, photographer*

# Cathedral Park

The Cathedral Park area, bounded on the north by Palace Avenue, on the west by Cathedral Place, on the south by ST. FRANCIS CATHEDRAL, and on the east by Marian Hall, was originally purchased on May 26, 1856, from José Francisco Baca y Terrus by Bishop Jean Baptiste Lamy for $1,000. Bishop Lamy sold this along with adjoining parcels to Sister Mary Vincent, Superior of the Sisters of Charity.

Cathedral Park is the site of the original St. Vincent Sanatorium that opened in 1883. An 1887 photograph shows the area enclosed by sandstone pillars, connected by an ornamental iron fence on top of a sandstone base. Two lower pillars framed a gate for pedestrians at the corner of Palace Avenue and Cathedral Place. By 1935 the corner had been

slightly rounded and the gate moved back to accommodate the widening of the sidewalk; however, the pillars and fence remain.

The first sanatorium was destroyed by fire in 1896, but twelve years later reconstruction was begun on the same site. This building was remodeled in 1954 for use as a convent and school for nurses, and renamed Marian Hall. Even with the church's extensive building program in the surrounding area throughout the years, the large park forming the southeast corner of Palace Avenue and Cathedral Place has, for about ninety years, been preserved as an open air space to be enjoyed by Santa Fe citizens. It forms an important piece of the fabric of the Santa Fe Historic District.

The CATRON business block signified commercial progress on the PLAZA.
*Vincent Foster, photographer*

# Catron Block

### East side of Plaza

This impressive business block was completed on the northeast corner of the PLAZA in 1891 for powerful lawyer and politician, Thomas Benton Catron. It was designed for stores on the first floor and offices on the second, and for many years Catron's office afforded him a commanding view of the PALACE OF THE GOVERNORS and the PLAZA. His large collection of books contained what was reputed to be the most extensive law library west of the Mississippi River.

A native of Missouri, Catron came to Santa Fe in 1866 at the age of twenty-six and entered the practice of law. Almost immediately he began his swift political rise that included appointment to the top judicial posts in the territory, a term as mayor of Santa Fe, four terms in the territorial legislature,

and that culminated with his election at the age of seventy-two to the United States Senate as one of New Mexico's first two senators after statehood.

Catron's name was long associated with leadership of the "Santa Fe Ring," a powerful and shifting alliance of primarily Republican political and business leaders, who for many years were said to control the business and political life of the territory. The "Ring" was particularly active in land grants and Catron himself was estimated to own millions of acres. Of the business ventures in which he was involved, perhaps the most successful was the formation of the region's first bank, The First National Bank of Santa Fe, which today is the oldest bank in the Southwest.

The Catron Block was built by the local firm of

Berardinelli and Palladino in the Italianate, or, as it is sometimes called, the railroad commercial style, which in this period represented to Santa Fe's business leaders the urgently needed modernization of the commerce district. Brick, stone, or cast iron facades, and large display windows were favored on the PLAZA; adobe and *portales* were scorned. Half a million bricks went into the construction of the Catron building, and forty thousand pressed bricks were ordered from the penitentiary for the front. A galvanized metal cornice and fifteen or more huge plate glass windows were shipped in from the East.

On the ground floor in 1912 Emil and Johanna Ulfelder opened the White House, offering Santa Fe's first ready-made fashions for women. After Emil's death, Johanna married Morris Blatt. In 1927, two years after Catron's death, the Blatts bought the building from the Catron heirs, and for many years it has been known as the Blatt building. Today it is owned by a family partnership headed by the Ulfelders' daughter, granddaughter, and grandson. The closing of the Guarantee in 1988 brought to an end seventy-six years of stores in the building owned and managed by Ulfelder descendants. Only a year earlier the law firm of Catron, Catron, and Sawtell, headed by Thomas Catron's grandsons, moved from the second floor to offices on the south side of town. However, the building's legal tradition continues; the law office of Emil Ulfelder's great-grandson occupies part of the second floor.

The exterior of the Catron Block has been altered at the ground level over the years. In the late 1960s a Territorial Revival *portal* was added. About ten years later large display windows were replaced by smaller windows of varying size and stucco was applied to suggest the contours and color of adobe. Nevertheless, on the second story, adobe-colored paint has not obscured the striking features of the building—the arrangement of pilasters and arched windows with exaggerated keystones, as well as the overhanging cornice with its dentils, ornamental brackets, and central pediment. The least altered of the buildings that faced the PLAZA in 1891, the Catron Block is today a unique reminder of the architecture that dominated the PLAZA in the late nineteenth century.

Main facade of the CRESPÍN HOUSE, which is at a right angle to East de Vargas and behind a tall adobe wall.
*Alan K. Stoker, photographer*

# Gregorio Crespín House

**132 East de Vargas Street (private residence)**

At the western end of the BARRIO DE ANALCO, this house was part of the property owned in 1747 by Gregorio Crespín, who sold it for 50 *pesos* to Bartolomé Márquez with its "lands and an apricot tree." Tree-ring specimens taken from *vigas* in the house indicate their cutting date as 1720–50, and thick adobe walls testify further to its antiquity. The Territorial trim was added in the nineteenth century.

The property was owned between 1850 and 1862 by Don Blas Roibal, whose son, Benito, sold it in 1867 to Don Anastacio Sandoval, for whom Sandoval Street was named. The house was described as containing five rooms, a *portal* and a *placita*, with

"free entry and exit on the north side." For many years it was known locally as the Van Stone House.

The land itself was part of a tract granted by General de Vargas to Juan de León Brito, a Tlaxcalan Indian who participated in the reconquest of 1693. This grant was later validated by Governor Domingo de Bustamante in 1728.

In the Affidavit of Expenses for the rebuilding of SAN MIGUEL CHAPEL in 1710, Juan and his brother, Diego Brito, are credited with a contribution, "as alms," of fifteen hundred adobe bricks for its construction, out of the twenty-one thousand that were used to complete the building.

CRISTO REY CHURCH, built in 1940, is one of the largest modern adobe structures.
*Karl Kernberger, photographer*

# Cristo Rey Catholic Church

## Upper Canyon Road

Although of recent construction, the parish Cristo Rey Catholic Church is a classic example of New Mexico mission architecture of the Spanish period. It was designed primarily as a fitting sanctuary for the great stone *reredos,* or altar screen, that had originally been in LA CASTRENSE on the PLAZA, and that was the most famous Spanish colonial work of ecclesiastical art created in New Mexico and the prototype for the many hand-hewn wooden altar screens of the early period. The church was built in commemoration of the 400th anniversary of Coronado's exploration of the Southwest.

One of the largest modern adobe structures in existence, the church was designed by Santa Fe architect John Gaw Meem and built by contractor Fred Grill in the spirit and tradition of the old Spanish missions, with parishioners doing much of the labor under professional supervision. The 180,000 adobe bricks that went into its construction were made in the traditional way from the soil on which the church stands, and much of the woodwork, including the hand-carved corbels, was done at the site from the architect's design.

The building was dedicated on June 27, 1940, by Archbishop Rudolphus Aloysius Gerken, who had made the first two adobe bricks for its construction.

One of these disappeared the night of the dedication, but the other is still lodged in the south tower.

The beautiful hand-carved *reredos* behind the altar was originally commissioned in 1760 by Governor Francisco Antonio Marín del Valle for the military chapel. Made of native white stone from a quarry near Jacona, it was carved and painted by Mexican artisans brought to Santa Fe by Governor Marín del Valle. The work was done within the old chapel on the PLAZA, as evidenced by chippings and small carved pieces of stone like that of the *reredos* which were found on the site when LA CASTRENSE was excavated in 1955.

The carved stone plaque of Our Lady of Light in half-relief that is embedded in the central panel was originally installed in the wall above the entrance to LA CASTRENSE. At the top of the *reredos* is the figure of God, and beneath Him a panel of Our Lady of Valvanera. Below this, St. James the Apostle is depicted on horseback, with St. Joseph on his right and St. John Nepomuk on his left. The lower left panel contains St. Ignatius Loyola, and the lower right St. Francis of Solano. The intricate design is similar to that found in sixteenth-century European and seventeenth-century Mexican churches, from which it was derived.

Interior of CRISTO REY CHURCH with stone *reredos* originally located in LA CASTRENSE.
*Laura Gilpin, photographer*

Curvilinear features of California Mission Revival style are evident in the elegant facade of CUTTING HOUSE.
*Vincent Foster, photographer*

# Bronson M. Cutting House

## 908 Old Santa Fe Trail (private residence)

Like so many who came to New Mexico in the first decades of the twentieth century seeking a cure for tuberculosis, Bronson M. Cutting recovered to play a major role in the history of his adopted state. At the time of his premature death, he had owned and aggressively run the *Santa Fe New Mexican* for twenty-three years and had gained a national reputation as a United States senator from New Mex-

ico. A Progressive, he had amassed a huge and devoted political following, especially among the majority Hispanic population, which enabled him to control the politics at various times of either of the state's major parties.

The younger son of an extremely wealthy, old New York family, Cutting found soon after his arrival in Santa Fe in 1910 that he would have to build his own home if he were to have the sort of living accommodations to which he was accustomed. Specifically, he had difficulty finding a house that was sufficiently large and contained more than one bathroom.

After a brief flirtation with the idea of an adobe house in the incipient Spanish Pueblo Revival style, Cutting hired Colorado Springs architect Thomas MacLaren, formerly of London, to build a California Mission Revival mansion of conventional materials. In 1910, with the Pueblo Revival movement barely under way, the Mission Revival style was still considered appropriate for Santa Fe by virtue of its generalized evocation of a Spanish Colonial past. The Bronson M. Cutting House is one of a few remaining examples from this brief period in the architectural evolution of Santa Fe. Other examples are the SALMON-GREER HOUSE and the 1914 addition to the ROSARIO CHAPEL.

Exceptionally elegant and well balanced in design, the house embodies the characteristic features of the Mission Revival style in the liberal use of arches around window and door openings, the orientation around a central courtyard, and the curvilinear gable that, in this case, rises in the center of the main facade and corresponds to the rise in the roof line over the vaulted ceiling of the living room. Called *Los Siete Burros*, The Seven Burros, the house had three bedrooms and four bathrooms (at a time when more than one bathroom was luxurious in Santa Fe and indoor plumbing not to be taken for granted), a large kitchen, butler's pantry, dining room, living room, library, two open sleeping porches (indispensable for the cure of tuberculosis), and a servants' wing.

After Cutting's death at the age of forty-seven in a 1935 airplane crash, the house was purchased from the estate by Jesus Baca, a long-time associate and friend. In the 1950s it was bought by the Archdiocese of Santa Fe and converted into an orphanage for girls, called *Las Huérfanas*, The Orphan Girls. In the late 1960s it became the home of a physician who used the servants' quarters for medical offices. Today it remains a residence with a law office in the servants' wing. The setting of the house has been altered in recent years by the sale and development of much of the acreage that once surrounded it. The garage close to the Old Santa Fe Trail was built in the same style as the house, but it has been remodeled beyond recognition and is now a dwelling. Nevertheless, despite changes in ownership and use, the house itself has undergone minor or tangential alterations, and it remains substantially as it was when Cutting lived there.

The carefully renovated home of Randall Davey
was originally a sawmill.
*Alan K. Stoker, photographer*

# Randall Davey House

## Upper Canyon Road (May be seen by appointment)

The property was part of the Talaya Hill grant given in 1731 to Manuel Trujillo. Far from the PLAZA in Spanish days, it was used only for grazing and woodcutting until the first sawmill in Santa Fe was built there by the U.S. army quartermaster in 1847 to provide lumber for FORT MARCY, then under construction. The main house still shows the stone walls and huge, hand-hewn timbers of the mill on the interior, carefully preserved by the late owner, Randall Davey, an artist of international reputation.

In 1852 the property was sold at public auction and was described as including one mile of river frontage, "one grist mill, one circular sawmill with extra gearing; the building for said sawmill is a good two story building, built for that purpose. Also two dwelling houses and one stable." The

47

highest bidder—at $500—was Colonel Ceran St. Vrain, a well-known trader and trapper from St. Louis. After some litigation over mortgages to St. Vrain by temporary operators of the mill, St. Vrain sold the mill machinery to Joseph Hersch and Isaiah Smith in 1856 to be moved to another site. In 1864 the mill and land came into the possession of Louis Gold, another local trader, who bought it from Benito Borrego and his wife, María del Carmen Martínez, and José Candelario Martínez. the Martínezes were descendants of Nicolás Ortiz III, a powerful figure of eighteenth-century Santa Fe.

By 1892 the Davey property was owned by Captain Candelario Martínez, a native of Santa Fe who enlisted in the First Infantry, New Mexico Volunteers, at the age of eighteen. He was promoted to captain when he recaptured United States mail from Kiowa and Comanche Indians on the plains and survived a gunshot wound suffered during the me-

lee. Martínez later became an attorney and held positions as postmaster and probate judge in Santa Fe. In 1906 a United States patent signed by President Theodore Roosevelt was issued for the property.

Randall Davey bought the stone mill and other buildings in 1920, and converted the two-story central section into his home where he lived for the next forty-four years. The remainder of the house was constructed of adobe in New Mexico Territorial style and includes Davey's studio, which is maintained as it was during his lifetime. In 1983 the Randall Davey Foundation gave the property to the National Audubon Society. A registered historic site, the house and studio are open for viewing by the public at specified hours and for group tours by appointment. For details contact the Randall Davey Audubon Center.

RANDALL DAVEY HOUSE interior. Note the traditional brick floor, corner fireplace, stone walls, and hand-adzed beams.
*Alan K. Stoker, photographer*

RANDALL DAVEY STUDIO, a separate adobe building constructed by the artist.
*Vincent Foster, photographer*

DELGADO HOUSE entry facade showing Territorial-style wooden porch on upper story and, unusual for Santa Fe, a stone basement.
*James B. De Korne, photographer*

# Felipe B. Delgado House

## 124 West Palace Avenue

An excellent example of local adobe construction modified by late nineteenth-century architectural detail, this house was built in 1890 by Felipe B. Delgado, socially prominent Santa Fe merchant, and remained in the possession of the Delgado family until 1970, when it was purchased and renovated by John Gaw Meem. In January 1980 he and his wife, Faith, donated the Delgado House to The

Historic Santa Fe Foundation to insure its continued preservation. The stone base was laid by masons who had helped build ST. FRANCIS CATHEDRAL. The balcony, window casings, and elaborate wooden trim show the same influence that caused the extensive remodeling of the PALACE OF THE GOVERNORS in the Victorian manner after the Civil War.

Don Felipe was a grandson of Captain Manuel

Delgado, founder of the Delgado family in New Mexico, who enlisted in the Royal Army of Spain in 1776 and came to New Mexico in 1778. Many members of the family—including four brothers of Felipe—became merchants and were prominent in public life.

Felipe Delgado was educated in St. Louis, Missouri. Later he operated a general store in Santa Fe and was one of the principal owners of mule and ox trains freighting over the Santa Fe Trail to Independence and the Camino Real to Chihuahua. His wife was Doña Lucía Ortiz, daughter of an-other prominent citizen and trader, Captain Gaspar Ortiz y Alaríd, for whom Don Gaspar Avenue and Ortiz Street in Santa Fe are named.

In 1877, when Don Felipe bought the land on which this house now stands, it was part of the picket line for cavalry horses and wagon trains at the end of the Santa Fe Trail. During his lifetime the house was the scene of great social activity typical of territorial days during the late nineteenth and early twentieth centuries. He is buried in ROSARIO CEMETERY.

First floor interior of DELGADO HOUSE.
*Vincent Foster, photographer*

DIGNEO-MOORE HOUSE, 1911.
*Bart Durham, photographer*

# Digneo-Moore House

**1233 Paseo de Peralta**

# Digneo-Valdés House

**1231 Paseo de Peralta (private residence)**

These handsome brick houses stand on the south side of Paseo de Peralta just across from the New Mexico State Capitol and are both former residences of Carlo Digneo. In excellent condition and showing superior craftsmanship throughout, they are interesting examples of turn-of-the-century architecture.

A leader of the local Italian colony, Carlo Digneo

came to Santa Fe in 1880 with his brother, Michelangelo. Here they joined a third brother, Genaro, and brother-in-law, Gaetano Palladino, skilled masons and stone cutters who had been recruited in the East to hasten the construction of ST. FRANCIS CATHEDRAL. Soon augmented by the arrival of Palladino's son-in-law, Michele Berardinelli, also a builder and contractor, the local Italians seem to have adapted rapidly to Santa Fe's diverse culture and played a significant role in the city's growth. The Digneos and their relatives formed various partnerships that were responsible for erecting many homes and public buildings throughout New Mexico and at a few locations in Colorado and West Texas.

In 1889 Carlo Digneo built his first residence at 132 East Manhattan Avenue, now 1231 Paseo de Peralta. Made of locally hand-moulded brick, the house originally consisted of four rooms resting on a sandstone foundation and was topped by a cross-gabled roof and corbeled brick chimneys. With its large bay window and Eastlake porch it was the height of the fashion during the Gay Nineties. Divided into parlor, dining room, master bedroom, and sitting room, the interior was decorated with carved wooden mantels over two small coal-burning fireplaces and other detailed woodwork characteristic of the nineteenth century. The kitchen and extra bedrooms were in the basement until the first addition, which included a bathroom, was added to the building's south end soon after 1900.

Here Digneo and his wife, Angela Damiani, es-

Stone quoins, DIGNEO-MOORE HOUSE.
*Bart Durham, photographer*

Fireplace, DIGNEO-VALDÉS HOUSE. Courtesy of Cultural Properties Review Committee, Historic Preservation Division, State of New Mexico.
*Horace Thomas, photographer*

DIGNEO-VALDÉS HOUSE, 1889. Courtesy of Cultural Properties Review Committee, Historic Preservation Division, State of New Mexico.
*Horace Thomas, photographer*

tablished their home and raised their family of six children until Angela's death in 1896. Nine years later Digneo married Magdalena Delgado, a daughter of Felipe B. Delgado, one of Santa Fe's most prominent merchants and businessmen.

In 1911 Carlo moved his family into a new two-and-a-half-story brick house just west of his older home, which he conveyed to his niece, Melinda Digneo de Valdés, and her husband, Felipe Valdés.

Now covered by a heavy mat of ivy, Digneo's second residence was larger and more imposing than his first. Embellished with granite quoins and covered with a pressed metal roof, it is a fine example of the dignity and conservatism that typify pre–World War I architecture.

Following Carlo Digneo's death in 1928, the house at 1233 Paseo de Peralta was rented for several years. In 1934 it was sold to E. P. Moore, a leading merchant whose men's store was a fixture on the PLAZA for many years.

Turn-of-the-century stonework in FAIRVIEW
CEMETERY.
*Vincent Foster, photographer*

# Fairview Cemetery

## Cerrillos Road

Fairview is Santa Fe's only non-Catholic pioneer cemetery. The Fairview Cemetery Company was started in 1884 by a group of Santa Fe citizens who, after raising $1,250, purchased 4.3 acres on Cerrillos Road for the cemetery. But mismanagement and lack of funds were problems from the start.

The founding directors were accused of fiscal irresponsibility and replaced in 1890. Unfortunately, the new board was not able to get the company's finances in order and in 1899 control, but not ownership, passed to the Woman's Board of Trade, an active civic group founded in 1892 to improve Santa Fe.

An independent Cemetery Committee was formed and was entirely self-supporting from the sale of lots and annual fees for the care of the plots. The women comprising the committee were excellent managers who ran Fairview efficiently. They did such a fine job of beautifying the grounds that Fairview became known as the most beautiful "God's Acre" in New Mexico—renowned for its trees, well-tended lawns, and flowering shrubs. The Cemetery Committee was headed by May Spitz for over three decades. In 1930 the property was deeded to the Woman's Board of Trade, after it had merged with the Santa Fe Woman's Club, and a perpetual-care trust fund was created. This fund, which received a percentage of all money from the sale of lots, eventually grew to $100,000.

When May Spitz died in 1974, so did the era of careful guardianship of the Fairview Cemetery. In 1978, after facing increasing problems in financing the operation, the Woman's Club deeded the cemetery to Santa Fe County. The county had trouble running the cemetery and even tried to give it back to the Woman's Club. Deterioration set in. The Fairview Cemetery Preservation Association was founded in 1982, and the cemetery was restored to some of its former beauty by this group. Today, the cemetery is an example of what can be done by dedicated citizens intent on preserving a place of historic importance.

# First Ward School

**400 Canyon Road**

The brick construction of FIRST WARD SCHOOL is unusual for CANYON ROAD.
*Bart Durham, photographer*

Standing at the corner of CANYON ROAD and García Street, the First Ward School is an imposing one-story brick building with a modified hip roof. Opened in 1906 it is a classic example of a turn-of-the-century schoolhouse.

The present structure replaced a large adobe building that was sometimes used as a dance hall. It was purchased in 1876 by the Santa Fe county school commission. Poorly lighted and cold in winter, this crude facility served the children of Santa Fe's east side until 1905 when an advisory committee declared it "a disgrace" and recommended its replacement. The architectural firm of I. H. and W. M. Rapp was chosen to design the new school and the construction contract was awarded to Carlo Digneo, one of Santa Fe's best-known builders. The school's original cost to the taxpayers of Santa Fe was $5,311.

Even though the school was the pride of the neighborhood when it opened its doors in September 1906, its importance was short-lived. Four years earlier, St. Francis School had begun classes for an ever-increasing enrollment of students, many of whom came from the First Ward. This resurgence of Santa Fe parochial schools made the new building on CANYON ROAD something of a white elephant and after three years it became evident that continued operation was not economically feasible. In 1928 the building was sold to Dr. Frank Mera for $5,000. Since its sale by the board of education, the former First Ward School has served at various times as the location of natural history and wildlife exhibits, and as a theater, an apartment house, an antique shop, and an art gallery.

# Ruins of Fort Marcy

## Northeast of Santa Fe

Aerial view of the RUINS OF FORT MARCY, showing the embattlement contours and the path to the Cross of the Martyrs.
*Todd Webb, photographer*

Atop a steep hill overlooking the city of Santa Fe from the northeast within 600 yards of the PLAZA lie the remains of Fort Marcy, first United States military post in the Southwest. Although never used, the massive adobe fort symbolized the power of the conquering nation in its expansion of territory to the Pacific Ocean during the Mexican War.

On August 19, 1846, one day after officially accepting the peaceful surrender of New Mexico from Acting Governor Juan Bautista Vigil y Alaríd, Brigadier General Stephen Watts Kearny ordered Lieutenants William H. Emory and Jeremy F. Gilmer to reconnoiter the city to determine the best location for a fort. They selected the obvious location that, as Lieutenant Emory described it, was "the only point which commands the entire town and which itself is commanded by no other." On August 23 work started on the fort, and in a report to Washington, Kearny suggested that it be named for William L. Marcy, secretary of war.

The fort was constructed in an irregular star shape "with adobe walls nine feet high and five feet thick." These walls were surrounded by a ditch eight feet deep and enclosed an area 270 feet by 80 feet. A log building in the compound was to serve as a powder magazine and a log blockhouse was built east of the gate for additional defense. Barracks, corrals, and other facilities were located adjacent to the PALACE OF THE GOVERNORS as they had been under Spain and Mexico.

Inspecting the military facilities of Santa Fe in 1853, Colonel J. K. F. Mansfield wrote: "This is the only real fort in the territory. . . . It is well planned and controls a city of about 1,000 population. The troops do not occupy this fort, but it can be occupied at short notice."

With U.S. authority firmly fixed in New Mexico, Fort Marcy on the hill was neglected and its name came to be applied to the military post that was established north of the PLAZA, ultimately covering the area now bounded by Federal Place and Washington, Palace, and Grant avenues. The seventeen acres of land of the old Fort Marcy reservation were transferred to the Department of the Interior in 1891 and sold at public auction to L. Bradford Prince. The ruins of the fort and the land surrounding them were sold to the city of Santa Fe in 1969. The downtown Fort Marcy was abandoned by the army in 1894.

Today, the remains of Fort Marcy on the hill consist of mounds of earth several feet high, tracing the outline of the adobe foundations. The indentations of the ditch are also visible. A paved walkway from Paseo de Peralta leads to the Cross of the Martyrs, located just below the ruins.

# Fort Marcy Officer's Residence

**(Edgar Lee Hewett House)**
**116 Lincoln Avenue**

Fort Marcy Officer's Residence, more recently known as the Hewett House, is one of two buildings remaining from the Fort Marcy Military Reservation created in 1868. The residence is one of six houses constructed in the early 1870s, back to back, on Lincoln and Grant Avenues for officers' use. The A. M. BERGERE HOUSE on Grant Avenue is the only other of the six houses to survive. Both buildings were extensively altered after 1916 to bring their appearance into conformity with the prevailing Spanish Pueblo Revival style.

Though built of adobe, the six Fort Marcy officers' residences were designed in a modified form of the army's standard "Plan C." All were two-story, L-shaped buildings with cross-gable, metal roofs. The exterior walls were adobe-plastered, but the cor-

HEWETT HOUSE entrance.
*Vincent Foster, photographer*

57

ners were scored to simulate dressed stone quoins. A porch supported by six squared posts ran across the entire front of each house.

On October 19, 1900, six years after the army abandoned the reservation, the secretary of the interior granted permission to John R. McFie, associate justice of the New Mexico territorial supreme court, to occupy the officer's residence at 116 Lincoln Avenue. Judge McFie and his family remained in the house until January 5, 1904, when the Fort Marcy Abandoned Military Reservation was conveyed to the city of Santa Fe, and subsequently to the Santa Fe board of education.

The officer's residence changed hands several times during the next twelve years until it was purchased for attorney Frank Springer in March 1916. Elected to the territorial councils of 1880–81 and 1901–02, Springer also served as a member of the board of regents of the Museum of New Mexico and was president of the managing board of the School of American Research (founded in Santa Fe in 1907 as the School of American Archaeology). In 1916, at his own expense, Springer had the Fort Marcy Officer's Residence modified into the prevailing Spanish Pueblo Revival style to serve as a residence for Dr. Edgar Lee Hewett, director of both the School of American Research and the Museum of New Mexico. Both Springer and Hewett were prime movers in the Revival movement, which sought to retain, restore, and re-create Santa Fe's distinctive historic architecture. On September 20, 1917, Springer gave the building to the School for which it served as headquarters from 1959 until 1972, when the New Mexico State Legislature passed an appropriation from the general fund to purchase the building for use by the Museum of New Mexico.

The handsomely proportioned PADRE GALLEGOS HOUSE.
*Ken Schar, photographer*

# Padre Gallegos House

### 227–237 Washington Avenue

Soon after 1857, José Manuel Gallegos, a colorful and controversial priest who had been defrocked by Bishop Lamy five years earlier, built this house as his residence. Padre Gallegos was one of the most important figures in the stormy history of mid-nineteenth-century New Mexico.

During and after the Civil War, part of the building was used as a rooming house. Included among its tenants was Major John Ayres, quartermaster at FORT MARCY, who lived in the house for eighteen years. For a short period, the first Episcopal Church in Santa Fe, known as "The Good Shepherd Mission," was located in the north wing. As the mission was established in 1868, the same year in which Padre Gallegos married Candelaria Montoya, a widow, it is probable that the wedding took place there. The marriage, performed by John Woart, who was chaplain of Fort Union, is the first entry in the parish register of the Episcopal Church of the Holy Faith in Santa Fe.

José Manuel Gallegos was born in Abiquiu, New Mexico, in 1815. His great-great-grandfather, José Luis Valdez, a native of Oviedo, Spain, had come to New Mexico as a colonist in 1693. After receiving his early education as a student of the rebellious Padre Martínez of Taos, José Manuel studied for the priesthood in Durango, Mexico, where he was ordained in 1840. He ministered to various Indian pueblos and in Albuquerque, and also served in the departmental assembly of New Mexico from 1843 to 1846. Some historians believe he was one of the ringleaders in an attempted revolt against the Americans in December 1846.

In 1851, while priest at San Felipe de Neri Church in Albuquerque, he was elected to the upper house of the first legislative assembly of the territory of New Mexico. His rebellion against church authorities began the same year with the arrival of Bishop Lamy. Having heard of Padre Gallegos's gambling, dancing, and consorting with *politicos*, Bishop Lamy sent Vicar-General Machebeuf to Albuquerque to replace him. When Padre Gallegos staged an open revolt, Bishop Lamy suspended him from ministering in the church. In a countermove, Padre Gallegos claimed he held deeds from the bishop of Durango to the priest's residence adjoining San Felipe de Neri Church. Although the documents were apparently forged, a suit instituted by Vicar-General Machebeuf was dismissed in 1856, probably by mutual consent.

In the interim Padre Gallegos was elected to the position of territorial delegate to the U.S. Congress in 1853 and was reelected in 1855. He served in this session only until July 1856, when he was unseated by Miguel A. Otero, who had contested the election. After moving to Santa Fe in 1857, Padre Gallegos served four terms as speaker of the house in the legislative assembly and two years as territorial treasurer. In 1868 he was appointed superintendent of Indian Affairs by President Andrew Johnson.

One more term in the U.S. Congress during 1871 to 1873 ended the political career of Padre Gallegos. When death came from a stroke in 1875, the *Daily New Mexican* called him "the most universally known man in the Territory." His funeral, which was held at St. Francis Cathedral, was one of the largest ever witnessed in the city of Santa Fe. He was buried in Rosario Cemetery, where his marble tombstone still stands.

The Padre Gallegos house was remodeled and at the same time restored to its original proportions in 1966–67. Twenty years later it was again restored after a major fire.

Central courtyard and well of the Padre Gallegos House.
*Karl Kernberger, photographer*

# García-Stevenson House

## 408 Delgado and 522 Acequia Madre (private residence)

On April 3, 1848, Antonio Maria Archuleta received $200 from Rafael García for this property, which already included a house of six rooms with a *portal*, an enclosed *placita*, and a corral. It was a rather substantial farmhouse in this rural area east and south of the PLAZA on land irrigated from the ACEQUIA MADRE, which still borders it on the north. Some of these rooms may remain in the present structure.

In 1850 Rafael García was forty-four years old and a farmer. He and his wife Josepha had ten children. The building was enlarged with the addition of rooms and was eventually divided among García family members, as was often the custom. The historic core of the house, which is essentially two linear files of rooms placed side by side, took this shape while it was in the García family.

Descendants of Rafael García owned the house until 1920. In that year the eastern portion was sold to Kate Chapman who bought the western portion a year later. The wife of artist Kenneth Chapman, Kate Chapman was a pioneer in the restoration of old adobe buildings. She did much of her work in partnership with Margretta Dietrich's sister, Dorothy Stewart. Perhaps best known are her prize-winning restorations of the JUAN JOSÉ PRADA HOUSE and the BORREGO HOUSE, both done for Dietrich.

In 1930 the entire García property was sold to Philip Stevenson, a socially conscious novelist and playwright who was an active participant in Santa Fe's art colony. His "Sure Fire: Episodes in the Life of Billy the Kid," written for the 1931 Fiesta, was long remembered. Like many others in the 1930s, Stevenson was attracted to Communism as a solution to the devastating economic problems of that era. After leaving Santa Fe about 1939, he wrote screenplays in Hollywood and continued to write plays and novels, including a trilogy of novels published under the pseudonym, Lars Lawrence. He died in 1965 while touring the Soviet Union.

Stevenson's former wife retained ownership of the house and lived in part of it until 1952 when she sold it to Thomas Brown. Brown divided the property and sold the two parts separately. In 1954 the eastern half was bought by Faith and John Gaw Meem and remodeled for Marianne Gebhardt. Gebhardt made it her home and established the well-known Children's Patio Day School in an L-shaped addition created along the Acequia Madre and Delgado Street by connecting an adobe outbuilding to the house. The pegs where the children hung their coats are still to be seen.

Over the years there have been several additions to the house and changes in the use of interior space. Nevertheless, the basic structure of the building and its essential elements remain.

The García-Stevenson House represents the evolution of a Spanish Pueblo style home, some parts of which may date from before 1848. The linear floor plan and such features as thick adobe walls, *vigas*, varying floor levels and ceiling heights, as well as various other details and irregularities, reveal the essential elements of the earliest style of domestic dwelling built by Europeans in Santa Fe.

GARCÍA-STEVENSON HOUSE, entered by a walkway across the ACEQUIA MADRE.
*Vincent Foster, photographer*

61

GROSS, KELLY AND COMPANY WAREHOUSE, a commercial structure in the Spanish Pueblo Revival style.
*Vincent Foster, photographer*

# Gross, Kelly and Company Warehouse

## West Manhattan Avenue

In 1913 Gross, Kelly and Company, one of the Southwest's largest wholesalers, opened a Santa Fe branch and erected this warehouse in the Santa Fe railroad yards. The building was the first commercial structure of its type in the Spanish Pueblo Revival style in New Mexico. It was one of the first buildings designed in that style by architect Isaac Hamilton Rapp and served as an important early example of the practical possibility of adapting the pre-American regional style to contemporary commercial use.

Gross, Kelly and Company had long played a major role in the commerce of the Southwest, providing a link between the railroad and the still-remote regions of Colorado and New Mexico. The company had begun in 1869 at Harker, Kansas, as Otero, Sellar and Company, a forwarding and commission house that moved its warehouse from one terminal point to the next as the railroad moved across Kansas and into Colorado and New Mexico. When the railroad reached Las Vegas, New Mexico, in 1879, the company established a permanent headquarters and began to build branches in other cities. Two years later it became Gross, Blackwell and Company, and in 1902 was renamed Gross, Kelly and Company at the time Harry Warren Kelly became president.

The company served the important function of expediting the transfer of eastern manufactured goods for the raw materials of the frontier. In an economy where cash was scarce, payment was often accepted in goods, such as livestock, wool, or hides that were, in turn, sold to eastern manufacturers or held in anticipation of more favorable prices. In this way the company provided a dependable market for local products. Gross, Kelly and Company also engaged extensively in other enterprises, such as lumbering and the finishing of livestock. Among the firm's landholdings was the old Pecos Grant, which included the site of the ruined Pecos pueblo and mission church. In 1920 the company deeded about eighty acres containing these ruins to the Archdiocese of Santa Fe, which was to transfer it to the School of American Research. Eventually it was deeded to the National Park Service and became the Pecos National Monument.

The Santa Fe Branch handled primarily staple groceries, patent medicines, light hardware, and farming supplies that were sold to merchants along the routes of the Denver and Rio Grande Railroad north from Santa Fe and the Santa Fe Railway south to Torrance. Local products, primarily wool, hides, pelts, grain, potatoes, and beans were bought from local producers, large and small.

Rapp based the overall form and design of the warehouse, a long rectangular building with flat roof, battered walls, and corner towers, on the mission churches that the Spanish Colonial friars convinced the Pueblo Indians to build. However, instead of traditional adobe, prison brick was used and rounded contours were created with concrete.

Rapp continued to develop the possibilities of the Spanish Pueblo Revival style in Santa Fe. He returned to the Spanish missions for the building he designed to represent New Mexico at the Panama California Exposition in San Diego in 1915. He repeated this design with modifications just off the PLAZA for the Museum of Fine Arts, dedicated in 1917. Other examples of his use of the style for large institutional buildings are La Fonda Hotel (1920) and two buildings for Sunmount Sanitorium (1914 and 1920).

Dramatic hillside residence known as the HAYT-WIENTGE MANSION, showing mansard roof. *Nancy Ellis, photographer*

# Hayt-Wientge Mansion

**620 Paseo de la Cuma (private residence)**

This striking landmark is one of the best surviving examples of Victorian architecture in New Mexico.

The adobe house southeast of the mansion was constructed sometime prior to 1877, and the mansion was built in 1882 by Walter V. Hayt, who had come to New Mexico Territory from New York about 1879. A prominent Santa Fe merchant, Hayt operated a store on San Francisco Street in cooperation with a partner and was later a dealer in books, stationery, toys, and notions.

The mansion is constructed of hand-moulded fired brick probably made where an *acequia* crossed the property to the south. This house and the HESCH HOUSE are the only two historic residences in Santa Fe with mansard roofs.

In 1888 Hayt sold the house to Christina F. Wientge, wife of Frederick W. Wientge, a jeweler from New Jersey. One of Wientge's best-known works is a small table of silver filigree inlaid with turquoise and other native stones, which he designed for the 1893 Columbia Exposition in Chicago. Wientge built a small adobe just north of the mansion for use as a jewelry shop.

A brick room was added to the northeast corner of the house in 1899. In the 1920s the front porch was extended along the west side, the stone terracing was constructed in front, and Wientge's former jewelry shop was incorporated into the main building.

The mansion was occupied by members of the family until the death of Wientge's daughter, Eve, in 1972. After use for a time as a children's day care school, the house was purchased by Michael and Susan Weber, whose work on the restoration has been carefully documented.

A memorable sight has been the Christmas Eve display of more than 800 *farolitos* on the house and entire hillside.

HESCH HOUSE, showing mansard roof and wood trim.
*James D. De Korne, photographer*

# Philip Hesch House

### 324–326 Read Street (private residence)

This two-story house was built in 1888 by Philip Hesch, a Canadian-born master carpenter of German extraction who had recently arrived in Santa Fe with his large family. Characterized by an imposing mansard roof and "carpenter style" exterior ornament, it is one of the few remaining late nineteenth-century structures in the city influenced by contemporary European architectural details.

The abstract for the property begins with the conveyance of a parcel of land from Charles Lerouge and his wife, María Rita García, to John Allen on May 12, 1869. During the next ten years, Allen and other buyers acquired much of the adjoining land for speculative purposes in anticipation of the construction of the Atchison, Topeka and Santa Fe Railroad spur from Lamy Junction. The addition thus assembled was originally designated as "Valuable Building Lots" on the Santa Fe city map of 1880, and the lots on which this house was built were numbered 258 and 259. This description of the property has been repeated in all later transactions.

After passing through several hands, the property was purchased from Annie H. Hull by Hesch on March 19, 1888, and construction was soon started on the house that was to serve as the family home for many years. In 1906 Philip Hesch deeded the house to his wife, Catherine, "in love and affection." Six years later, the property was sold to Arthur G. Whittier, and Mr. and Mrs. Hesch moved to California. Some of their descendants, however, still live in Santa Fe. The property has changed hands several times since 1912.

The house is of frame construction, and originally the second story was shingled. In recent years, however, the exterior has been completely stuccoed. The interior on the east side has been remodeled, but the western portion, which contains a handsome carved wooden staircase and much of the original woodwork, remains as it was built.

HESCH HOUSE, original newel post and staircase. *James B. De Korne, photographer*

The retaining wall in front of the house is of stone left over from the building of St. Francis Cathedral and is similar in architectural treatment.

The land on which the house was built was part of a property that once included Martínez Street, the site of the present hotel La Posada, and East Palace Avenue itself, which before 1870 extended only to the eastern end of Sena Plaza. Beyond that were open fields and a path leading along the irrigation ditch known as Acequia de la Loma.

The property was acquired at intervals between 1856 and 1872 by Doña Francisca Hinojos, daughter of Blas Hinojos, who was Commandante Principal of New Mexico when he was killed during the 1835 Navajo campaign. In 1887 she bequeathed it to her son, Don Alfredo Hinojos, a prominent political figure, who was organist at St. Francis Cathedral for almost fifty years.

The small rear building with a hutch roof was formerly the kitchen for the main house.

The exterior detailing of the Hinojos House, unusual for adobe construction.
*James B. De Korne, photographer*

# Francisca Hinojos House

### 355 East Palace Avenue

Designed and constructed by itinerant French artisans who were brought here from Louisiana by Bishop Lamy to build St. Francis Cathedral, this late nineteenth-century residence is of special interest because of its unusual architectural detail. Although it is built of adobe, its exterior design and roof are more typical of Louisiana's architecture during French occupation than of Santa Fe's.

The trim of the interior doors, windows, and Territorial fireplaces is also of interest, for it typifies the period when craftsmen excelled in imitating such grained woods as mahogany, oak, and bird's-eye maple, in this case on woodwork of native pine.

Hinojos House interior.
*Karl Kernberger, photographer*

New Mexican and European construction features blend in ARCHBISHOP LAMY'S CHAPEL. Courtesy of Museum of New Mexico. Neg. No. 68292. *T. Harmon Parkhurst, photographer*

# Archbishop Lamy's Chapel

## Bishop's Lodge Road

This modest structure was built in the foothills north of Santa Fe by the first bishop of New Mexico, Jean Baptiste Lamy, in the late 1860s or early 1870s to serve as his private retreat.

The busy prelate, faced with the problems of an extensive jurisdiction and frequently beset with controversy, felt it imperative to find a retreat where he could periodically take brief refuge from the cares of his office. This he found along the Little Tesuque stream.

Sometime during the 1860s Bishop Lamy purchased for $80 a piece of land within the outer boundaries of the claimed, but never confirmed, Río de Tesuque Grant from Natividad Romero and his wife, Maria Vitalia García, residents of the Río de Tesuque settlement. The deed was not recorded until October 23, 1874. The title to the land can be traced to 1752 when it was owned by Juan de Ledesma.

The site was ideal for a retreat. The irrigation system was in place and the land productive. On the hillside the bishop built his "lodge," which he named Villa Pintoresca, obviously for the magnificent view. It was an unpretentious building, but then Bishop Lamy was an unpretentious cleric. Undoubtedly he supervised the construction himself, and the result was a combination of traditional Hispanic New Mexican and European architectural features. The lodge consisted of two small rooms, a bedroom and a sitting room, one on the north, the other on the south, separated by a hallway that led into the tiny chapel on the east. In the chapel he conducted his personal devotions and celebrated Mass for frequent guests.

The adobe walls were laid upon stone foundations (now covered with cement) and were mud-plastered on both the interior and exterior, as they are today. The gable ends, however, were of wood, and the pitched roofs were apparently shingled from the beginning. A graceful steeple, with a plain wooden cross atop its spire, rose above the roof. A *portal* extended around the west and south sides.

Bishop Lamy was a horticulturalist of no mean ability. His garden and orchard around his Santa Fe residence was a showplace. In his lush valley retreat along the Little Tesuque, with its abundance of water supplied by an old *acequia,* he planted gardens and set out shrubs and fruit trees, many of which were imported from France. Some are still bearing fruit. There may actually have been a few apricot and peach trees on the property when he bought it. One account speaks of a wagon load of peaches from his land taken to Santa Fe in 1873.

With Bishop Lamy's death in 1888 the land and chapel became the property of Archbishop Salpointe whose successor, Archbishop Chapelle, filed a claim for the property in 1896. On March 20, 1900, Bishop Chapelle was issued a patent on 152.8 acres. There is no evidence that any of Bishop Lamy's successors actually occupied the living quarters of the retreat, but the chapel remained in use.

In 1909 the property was deeded by Archbishoip Pitaval to Carl Stephan. During the next few years there were several owners, including members of the Pulitzer publishing family. Deed restrictions covered the use of the chapel. In 1918 the property was sold to James R. Thorpe II, a Colorado businessman. It has remained in the Thorpe family ever since and has been developed into a resort known as The Bishop's Lodge.

The restrictions concerning the chapel were no longer part of the deed, but the Thorpe family has faithfully preserved and protected it for the benefit of visitors by retaining its exterior intact and rehabilitating the interior, which had fallen into disrepair. Some minor changes have been made, but none alters the building's integrity. The present *vigas* appear to have replaced former rafters in ceiling construction. The floor of the hallway has been cemented, but the other rooms still have wood floors. Most of the doors are original, as is the hardware. And, the simple, painted altar was probably placed there by Bishop Lamy.

Much of the interior work seems to have been done in 1928 under the supervision of Santa Fe artist Carlos Vierra and New Mexico writer and tour guide Erna Fergusson, then a hostess at the Lodge. On July 29 of that year Fergusson invited her friend Willa Cather, author of *Death Comes for the Archbishop*, to the Lodge as a guest, partly to see the chapel that she and Vierra were responsible for "restoring."

Today, the simple, little chapel built more than a century ago by a French prelate as a place to pray and retreat from the cares of an ecclesiastical jurisdiction still welcomes visitors for a few moments of peace and reflection.

Main facade of LORETTO CHAPEL.
*Vincent Foster, photographer*

# Loretto Chapel

### 219 Old Santa Fe Trail

The world-famous stone chapel of the Sisters of Loretto, known as "The Chapel of Our Lady of Light," was constructed as part of Archbishop Jean Baptiste Lamy's ambitious church building project that culminated in ST. FRANCIS CATHEDRAL. Loretto Chapel was designed to serve the spiritual needs of the nuns and students of the academy for girls

that had been founded in January 1853, shortly after Bishop Lamy had brought six sisters of the Order of Loretto to New Mexico.

Bishop Lamy turned over his own two-story adobe residence for the sisters' use, and their first chapel was located there. From 1859 to 1863 the Order acquired the large block of land on which their school, convent, and chapel were finally located. During the Confederate invasion of 1862, the nuns feared for the safety of their charges, and Bishop Lamy appealed to the military commander and secured protection of the institution.

Under the direction of the younger member of a French father-and-son team named Mouly, masons began cutting the stone on January 19, 1874. After many interruptions, the delicately proportioned Gothic Revival chapel, with its rose window, was blessed by Vicar-General Peter Eguillon on April 25, 1878. The ten-foot-high iron statue of Our Lady of Lourdes was placed on the pinnacle of the building ten years later. The Gothic Revival altar and communion railing were made in Italy around the turn of the century and are of carved wood painted to resemble white marble.

When the chapel was completed, there was no means of ascending to the choir loft, since the workmen felt that there was insufficient room to build a safe staircase. The sisters sought someone who could devise a stairway. Shortly thereafter, a carpenter appeared and constructed the famous circular staircase, built without nails or other visible means of support. He then disappeared without waiting to be paid. Legend has persisted that it was the work of St. Joseph, the carpenter saint. One of the several European artisans living in Santa Fe at the time may have been the unknown carpenter, but recent information strongly suggests the possibility that the craftsman was Johann Hadwiger, an Austrian immigrant who had heard of the sisters' quest while visiting his son in a Colorado mining camp. The "miraculous" nature of the staircase

1867 French harmonium bearing the inscription: For Bishop Lamy, Santa-Fé, New-Mexico.
*Vincent Foster, photographer*

Rose window of LORETTO CHAPEL.
*James B. De Korne, photographer*

is in no way dimmed by the probability of human construction.

The extensive property of the Sisters of Loretto was sold in 1971 for commercial development. The chapel has been maintained as a historic site by its owners, The Inn at Loretto.

In 1982, through the diligent efforts of organist Mary J. Straw and with assistance from the Foundation, the chapel's harmonium was restored and returned to its historic place in the choir loft. This keyboard instrument, whose sound is produced when metal reeds are vibrated by air forced from the two pedal-operated bellows, was made in 1867 by Alexandre François Debain of Paris who held the title, *"Inventeur de l'Harmonium."* Above the expression knob is an engraved brass plaque stating, "For Bishop Lamy, Santa-Fé, New-Mexico."

The famous "miraculous stairway" of Loretto Chapel.
*James B. De Korne, photographer*

MANDERFIELD MAUSOLEUM, ROSARIO CEMETERY.
*Bart Durham, photographer*

# Manderfield Mausoleum

## Rosario Cemetery

One of Santa Fe's leading nineteenth-century newspapermen, William H. Manderfield, was born in Berks County, Pennsylvania, June 16, 1841. As a young man he became a printer and subsequently made his way west, plying his trade at various locations in Illinois, Missouri, and Colorado before coming to Santa Fe. Here he found employment as shop foreman on *The Santa Fe New Mexican*, then a four-page weekly half in English and half in Spanish. Soon after his arrival in 1863, Manderfield purchased the paper from Charles P. Clever, and the following year he formed a management partnership with Thomas S. Tucker. Although plagued by delinquent subscribers and an untrained work force, together they made this newspaper one of the Southwest's leading journals. It championed the cause of the Union, the "Santa Fe Ring," and free public schools.

On October 13, 1870, both Tucker and Manderfield were married to daughters of well-known Santa Fe families in ceremonies conducted by Bishop Jean Baptiste Lamy. Tucker's bride was María Trinidad Ortiz; Manderfield wed Josefa Salazar.

In 1881 *The Santa Fe New Mexican* was sold to E. B. Purcell of Manhattan, Kansas. This permitted Manderfield to devote his time to horticulture and local politics.

Upon Manderfield's death seven years later, a handsome mausoleum was erected in ROSARIO CEMETERY. Constructed of dressed sandstone and embellished with squared pillars and stained glass windows, it remains today as a monument to this pioneer editor and his family. Threatened with demolition in 1979 because of vandalism, the structure has been stabilized and protected by The Historic Santa Fe Foundation.

# The "Oldest House"

### 215 East de Vargas Street

The origins of this house seem to be lost, but for more than a century tradition has called it the oldest house in Santa Fe. It was labeled the "oldest building" in the city on the Stoner map of 1882, and the Urrutia map of 1766–68 shows a structure near the CHAPEL OF SAN MIGUEL in the approximate position of this house. Tree-ring specimens, taken from some of the *vigas* in the ceilings of the lower rooms, show cutting dates of 1740–67.

On July 31, 1881, the house, although not specifically mentioned in deeds of title, was sold for $3,000 by Bishop Lamy to the Brothers of the Christian Schools, popularly known as the Christian Brothers, with the CHAPEL OF SAN MIGUEL and other property. For decades this house was included in descriptions pertaining to the area immediately surrounding the CHAPEL OF SAN MIGUEL.

The house had two stories in nineteenth-century photographs and paintings. In 1902 when the building was badly in need of repair, the second story was removed. The house remained a one-story structure until about a quarter of a century later, when a new second story was added. Presently, the eastern portion is rented as a curio shop, while the western part remains a unique remnant of the type of building once prevalent in the city—part Indian, part Spanish, low-ceilinged and crude, with dirt floors and thick adobe walls.

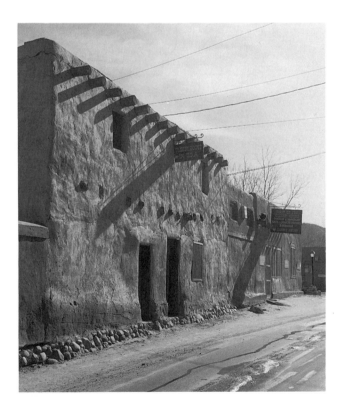

The "OLDEST HOUSE."
*Karl Kernberger, photographer*

The "OLDEST HOUSE" interior.
*Karl Kernberger, photographer*

NICOLÁS ORTIZ III HOUSE.
*Vincent Foster, photographer*

# The Ortiz Property

**306–308 and 322¹/₂ West San Francisco Street**

In the late 1700s these two structures formed the eastern and western sections of the Santa Fe hacienda of Antonio José Ortiz, on property which extended south to present Water Street and westward beyond what is now Jefferson. The house at 322¹/₂ is the older portion and had been the residence of his father, Nicolás Ortiz III. It is clearly depicted on the Joseph de Urrutia map of 1766, which also shows the same street pattern for San Francisco that now exists. How much older than 1766 the Nicolás Ortiz house may be is not known, but its thick adobe walls are more than 200 years old.

The Ortiz family is one of the most famous "first families" of New Mexico. Nicolás I came with General de Vargas as a civilian colonist in 1693. His son, Nicolás II, was a military man and held important civil posts. Nicolás III, son of Nicolás II, was captain of the Santa Fe presidio when he was killed August 31, 1769, in a skirmish with the Comanche near San Antonio Mountain. When Governor Pedro Fermín de Mendinueta called upon Ortiz's widow, Josefa

Bustamante, at her home to offer his condolences, she sadly remarked that such evils happened in New Mexico because there was "no sworn Patron Saint." The governor and the widow decided to hold a public celebration in honor of Our Lady of the Rosary, "La Conquistadora," for intercession to protect New Mexico from further Indian attack. The celebration, held in 1770, is the first documented Santa Fe Fiesta since 1712, when the city council had decreed an annual fiesta in honor of the twentieth anniversary of de Vargas's first expedition to reconquer New Mexico.

In 1771 Nicolás's son, Antonio José, and five others formed a committee to perpetuate the program. By 1776 the fiesta was a three-day affair, beginning with vespers the preceding evening, followed by masses, religious processions, theatrical performances and games, with government officials in attendance at all events, escorted by the royal garrison firing salvos. Citizens set *luminarias* for the occasion. This description is very similar to today's Santa Fe Fiesta.

Antonio José Ortiz was one of the largest land-owners in New Mexico, with ranches, including one at Pojoaque, and extensive grazing lands. An important trader between Santa Fe and Mexico, he maintained a twelve-room dwelling in El Paso for the use of his family and agents on trading trips. He contributed to the building of SANTUARIO DE GUADALUPE and ROSARIO CHAPEL, the repair of SAN MIGUEL CHAPEL, La Conquistadora chapel, and the parish church of St. Francis.

Antonio José enlarged the original Santa Fe home to include a section at 306–308 West San Francisco. This portion of the property was extensively altered in a remodeling performed in 1972 under the Urban Renewal program when this property became part of the Hilton hotel.

In 1855 the Ortiz family property came into the hands of Anastacio Sandoval, merchant, colonel in the New Mexico militia during and after the Civil War, territorial treasurer in 1864, auditor in 1867, adjutant general in 1871, and member of the territorial legislature for sixteen years. The street that bears his name was apparently laid out shortly after the purchase, and he used the eastern section on the corner of San Francisco and the new street, built by Antonio Jośe Ortiz, as headquarters for his large mercantile establishment. In 1870 Sandoval conveyed this portion to Pedro Aranda. This land subsequently changed hands several times.

The next year, Sandoval also sold the original Nicolás Ortiz house at 322$^1/_2$ West San Francisco. After a succession of owners, the older portion was purchased by the Abeytia family of Socorro in 1884. In the early 1970s these buildings were included in the area that underwent "urban renewal."

Through changes of fortune and use, the two buildings are no longer as imposing as they once were, when, within their walls, governors, bishops, and military visitors were entertained, New Mexico policies decided, and the Santa Fe Fiesta revived.

NICOLÁS ORTIZ III HOUSE facade detail.
*Peter Dechert, photographer*

# Palace of the Governors

PALACE OF THE GOVERNORS, south main entrance facade and *portal*, across from the PLAZA. *Karl Kernberger, photographer*

The Palace of the Governors, constructed in 1610 following the establishment of the Villa of Santa Fe by Governor Pedro de Peralta, is the oldest public building in the United States that has been in continuous use. Originally, the royal houses and grounds ran from the PLAZA north to the site of the present federal buildings and contained the governor's private apartments, official reception rooms and offices, military barracks, stables, arsenal, and servants' quarters. Vegetable gardens were planted in a central patio consisting of some ten acres. The Palace extended farther to the west in Spanish times and had two *torreones*, or defense towers, on the east and west corners of the facade. The western tower served as a prison and for storage of gunpowder. No *portal* existed.

During the Pueblo Revolt of 1680, the troops and refugees gathered within the Palace and resisted attacks until the Indians, after a ten-day siege, cut off the water supply and forced the Spaniards to retreat to the El Paso region. During the next twelve years, the Indians pulled down the houses and the

parish church and used the adobe bricks to fortify the Palace. Upon his reconquest in 1693, General de Vargas found that the building had only one or two entrances, no outside windows, four or five defensive towers, and walls around the whole complex. Within, the Indians had subdivided the Spanish rooms into typical Indian cubicles with thin, puddled partitions, remains of which still exist in some interior walls.

Turning the tables on the rebels, de Vargas also cut off the water supply from the springs to the east and forced the Indians to surrender after some days of bloody attacks on the fortress. The governor, soldiers, colonists, and priests all lived in the Palace until other housing could be provided. For want of a chapel, de Vargas had the Franciscans purify and bless the east *torreón*, which the Pueblos had made into a pagan *kiva*. When de Vargas died in 1704, there was still no principal church, and it is probable that he was buried in the floor of the *torreón* chapel, which then extended out into the PLAZA and Washington Street. After the parish

77

church was built in 1714, the *torreones* on the Palace were torn down in order to straighten the Plaza. When the southeastern room was excavated in 1965, the foundations of the east *torreón* were clearly visible, but no remains of de Vargas were found. His bones may still lie under the passing traffic of that busy street corner.

The Palace as the seat of government saw such distinguished incumbents as Marín del Valle, who built the military chapel with its stone altar screen, and Juan Bautista de Anza, who, after founding the city of San Francisco in California, was sent to New Mexico as governor and saved the province from near extermination at the hands of the Comanche. The visit of Bishop of Durango Pedro de Tamarón in 1760 was celebrated by a reception in the Palace and procession to the parish church. In 1807 Lieutenant Zebulon M. Pike was interrogated in the Palace after he and his few companions had been arrested on the headwaters of the Rio Grande.

Mexican governors continued to occupy the building for official business and private residence. At different times rooms were used for different purposes; what was once a *sala*, or reception and ballroom, or perhaps a governor's apartment, was later a council room or library. On August 18, 1846, Brigadier General Stephen Watts Kearny occupied the Palace in the name of the United States. Confederate forces used it as headquarters for a few weeks in 1862.

In time the Palace was outgrown and a territorial capitol was built across the Santa Fe River. This capitol was later burned and rebuilt. The original building was still used for offices, but was in such sad condition that the territorial government threatened to tear it down, only to be stopped by the protests of public-spirited citizens. The 1909 legislature appropriated funds to convert it into the Museum of New Mexico, and remodeling for this purpose was completed in 1913. The graceful, scroll-saw *portal* of 1878 was replaced by the present one of earlier Spanish style, but Victorian doors and windows were retained. The Palace exhibits include prehistoric archaeology materials, as well as those from Spanish, Mexican, and United States periods.

Entry *placita* of the DE LA PEÑA HOUSE, notable for its deep *portal* and second-story balcony.
*Vincent Foster, photographer*

# De la Peña House

**(Frank G. Applegate House)**
**831 El Caminito (private residence)**

Noted for its early nineteenth-century Spanish Pueblo architecture on both the exterior and interior, this house was occupied for almost eighty years by the de la Peña family, for whom Calle Peña was named. The Historic American Building Survey of 1941, edited by the National Park Service, lists the house as one of the eight Santa Fe buildings of historical importance to the United States, and photographs of it taken in 1937 are in the Library of Congress.

The earliest date of record for the property is May 3, 1845, when it was sold by Tomás de Jesús López to Sergeant Francisco de la Peña for 114 *pesos*. It was described as a piece of farmland with a "house of four rooms and a *portal* situated in said land." The original east *portal*, which contains a shep-

herd's bed, is now an enclosed room. The property transfer of 1845 subsequently involved "agricultural land" and referred to numerous *acequias* on or bordering the property. None of these runs today.

Sergeant de la Peña was a regular army soldier who served in the presidial companies of both Santa Fe and San Miguel before being mustered out June 18, 1846. He was with the military force that negotiated a peace treaty with the Navajo in 1835 and participated in two campaigns against the Indians, as well as one against the Texas Expedition of 1841 for which he received the Shield of Honor award.

When Francisco de la Peña died in 1887, he left his wife, Isabelita Rodríguez de la Peña, and eight children. After her death the property was divided in 1909 among the six surviving children, each receiving a portion of the land, six *vigas* of the house, and free entrance and exit to it. Two daughters were still living there in 1925.

In 1925 and 1926 Frank G. Applegate purchased the house and land from the surviving Peña heirs. He enlarged the house, built the second story, and had the beam, which was on the front *portal*, raised to that level and a copy of it installed on the first floor *portal*. Authentic details incorporated into the house at that time were Spanish Colonial balconies, taken from an old building, three old New Mexican *alacenas* built into the walls, squared beams, and corbels. Some of the walls are three feet thick in the four original rooms, two of which are combined in the present living room.

Applegate, who died in 1931, was a well-known writer and artist and one of the first leaders in Santa Fe to take a major interest in local crafts. He and the writer Mary Austin were active in organizing a group that provided funds for the repair of the church at Las Trampas and the mission churches of Ácoma, Laguna, and Zia. The group also purchased the Santuario de Chimayó, then a private chapel, and after restoring it, gave it to the Catholic Church.

In addition to his other accomplishments, Applegate had architectural training and was a leader in the movement among artists who came to Santa Fe in the 1910s and 1920s to develop an architecture based on Spanish Colonial and Pueblo Indian traditions. He designed renovations of several other old dwellings, designed new ones, and helped other artists, most notably those called *Los Cinco Pintores*, design and build traditionally styled adobe houses. His work was characterized by exceptional diversity and attention to detail and helped to define the Spanish Pueblo Revival style.

The shepherd's bed fireplace, a distinctive feature of the DE LA PEÑA HOUSE.
*Vincent Foster, photographer*

# The Plaza

Originally a rectangle reaching east as far as the present cathedral, the Plaza has always been the heart of Santa Fe. During the establishment of the city as a villa in 1610, it was laid out as the usual Spanish *plaza mayor*, designed for military and religious functions and therefore made "at least half again as long as its width, because this form is best for celebrations with horses." On the north side stood the *casas reales* or PALACE OF THE GOVERNORS, and on the other three were built the homes of prominent citizens. The Plaza served as the setting for daily markets, chicken pulls, cockfights, and other social gatherings, as well as for the public stocks and flogging post. The town crier used it to make public proclamations.

The Plaza was the central scene for the Pueblo Revolt of 1680 in which the Indians successfully besieged the Spaniards barricaded within the Palace, then allowed them to retire to El Paso del Norte. General de Vargas triumphantly rode into it twice, once on the reconnoitering expedition of 1692, and again in 1693 to reconquer the Kingdom of New Mexico. Because the Indians had razed the buildings, except for the Palace, which they had fortified, Santa Fe was rebuilt.

Encroachment on the Plaza began at an early period although Governor Cruzat y Góngora had decreed that streets should be made and kept at the width of eight *varas* (approximately twenty-two feet). In the 1740s the governor bought a house in order to demolish it because it obstructed the entrance to the parish church. In 1756 Governor Marín del Valle ordered certain citizens to open the streets upon which they had encroached with fences and buildings, especially "in front of the house of this Royal Presidio." By 1800, however, the Plaza had been greatly reduced in size.

With Mexican independence from Spain in 1821, the Plaza was renamed the Plaza of the Constitution. In the late 1820s a rock sundial was set up on a nine-foot adobe base in the center of the Plaza as "the only public clock to guide the authorities and employees." It bore the inscription *Vita fugit sicut umbra* (Life flees like a shadow).

From 1821 to the arrival of the railroad the Plaza was the end of the Santa Fe Trail, and caravans of Yankee merchandise were unloaded at the customs house on the east side. Since it was also the terminus for the Chihuahua Trail, the Plaza was an interlocking of two great trade routes.

A bullring stood in the Plaza for a short time in 1844 but was torn down after Ute Indians held it to ambush Governor Martínez de Lejanza in the Palace. In 1846 General Kearny proclaimed the annexation of New Mexico by the United States, with himself as military governor, to the citizens assembled in the Plaza.

For a few weeks in 1862 Confederate forces occupied Santa Fe, and their flag flew over the Plaza before their defeat at the battle of Glorieta forced them to retreat to Texas. The obelisk in the center of the Plaza commemorates New Mexico's defenders against both hostile Indian attack and Confederate invasion, and is probably the only monument to Union forces south of the Mason and Dixon line. In territorial days the Plaza had a white picket fence around it and a gingerbread wooden bandstand where concerts were given by the Fort Marcy band.

The Plaza of Santa Fe was declared a National Historic Landmark in 1962. Since that year, the commercial buildings on its three sides, all erected within the past century, have been unified by *portales* over the facades.

View of the PLAZA, looking north to the PALACE OF
THE GOVERNORS.
*Karl Kernberger, photographer*

Stone POWDER HOUSE, one mile south of the PLAZA.
*Vincent Foster, photographer*

# Powder House

## Galisteo Street

At the beginning of the 1880s many Santa Feans believed that their part of New Mexico was on the verge of a mining boom. Reports of rich gold and silver strikes in the Cerrillos district led to a feeling that mineral development at Carbonateville, Bonanza City, and other camps now long forgotten would make the southern part of the county one of the territory's great mining centers.

Plaza merchants were well aware that exploitation of the resources at Cerrillos and elsewhere would bring a strong demand for mining equipment and supplies, including blasting powder. But because of its unstable composition, stocking that item presented a difficult storage problem. To prevent explosive disasters in Santa Fe, representatives of the aptly named Hazard Powder Company, a Connecticut corporation, sought a suitable location for an explosives repository well away from the center of town. On July 3, 1880, the company purchased from leading businessman James L. Johnson a one-acre lot east of the Galisteo road and a mile south of the PLAZA. Although the old road has turned into busy Galisteo Street and the location is now part of a residential neighborhood, in 1880 the only structure nearby was Johnson's slaughterhouse, which stood a few hundred yards to the west. Using rough-dressed, native sand-

stone, local masons constructed a small pitch-roofed building suitable for storing powder. A heavy wooden door reinforced with sheet iron formed the entrance, the only opening in the eighteen-inch thick walls.

One of Santa Fe's best-known mercantile houses, Spiegelberg Brothers, acted as agent for the Hazard Company and assumed responsibility for managing the Powder House. As part of a corporate reorganization, the Hazard Company transferred title to the Powder House to a subsidiary of E.I. Du Pont de Nemours Company in 1909. For the next thirty years the chemical and explosives giant retained ownership of the building while local hardware dealers looked after its operation. In 1939 the property was purchased by a Santa Fe mining man, Joseph Byrne, who also owned a trucking company and a petroleum distribution business. Subsequently, the Church of Jesus Christ of Latter-day Saints acquired the property that included the little building and later conveyed it to its present owner, the Unitarian Church of Santa Fe. At various times the Powder House has been threatened with destruction but fortunately it remains today to recall the boundless optimism that characterized the hardy miners of New Mexico's frontier.

The PRADA HOUSE boasts a brick parapet and
windows at street level.
*Alan K. Stoker, photographer*

# Juan José Prada House

## 519 Canyon Road (private residence)

According to early maps, this house may have been in existence as early as 1768, although its first date of record is over 100 years later. In 1869, when it was owned by Juan José Prada, it consisted of two sections, with a corridor running from north to south between them. At that time, he deeded the west section to Altagracia Arrañaga, and in 1882 his widow deeded the east section to her son-in-law, Miguel Gorman, a descendant of one of the soldiers in the U.S. Army of Occupation. The deeds stipulated that the front door of the corridor be left open to allow access to a dance hall in the rear, and that the well in front of the house, which is still standing, was to be free for the use of those living in both sections. During the late nineteenth century the brick *pretil*, or coping, was added to the roof by artisans who built ST. FRANCIS CATHEDRAL.

In 1927 the east wing was purchased as a residence by the late Margretta S. Dietrich, who added other rooms and modernized its interior without changing its classic Territorial style of architecture. Later, she acquired the west section of the house and joined the two together, but without the original connecting corridor.

Still intact at the northern end of the property is a small barn of *jacal* construction—squared-off cedar logs more than thirty inches in circumference set upright in the ground with cracks chinked with adobe (picture on page 12). This type of construction was often used in New Mexico.

The first owner of record, Juan José Prada, was a descendant of José Prada, a native of Chihuahua, who came to Santa Fe as a soldier in the Santa Fe garrison of the Spanish army.

Queen Anne–style exterior of the 1886 PRESTON HOUSE. The brick has been stuccoed, and the metal roof simulates tile. Courtesy of Cultural Properties Review Committee, Historic Preservation Division, State of New Mexico.

# George Cuyler Preston House

**106 Faithway Street**

The George Cuyler Preston House, an excellent example of Queen Anne architectural style, is probably the only such residence extant in Santa Fe. The first date of record associated with the land upon which the house sits is February 21, 1865, when it was sold to Francisca Hinojos for $500.

On November 30, 1885, the land was conveyed to George Cuyler Preston, a law partner of Charles H. Gildersleeve, a leading New Mexico Democrat and member of the politically powerful "Santa Fe Ring."

Preston constructed his palatial three-story brick and frame home facing Palace Avenue in 1886. It was built on a stone foundation supporting fired bricks that are now hidden by a coat of stucco. The second story is clad with sheets of pressed metal, not with wood shingles as it first appears. The roofing is also metal. A large letter P on the main chimney has been attributed to Preston but may date only from the later occupancy of Dr. Louis E. Polhemus, the hygienist, herbalist, and dietician.

The Prestons speculated in building lots in the Santa Fe area, using their home as collateral. After they defaulted on a bank loan, the Second National Bank took possession of the house, but by this time the Prestons had moved to Denver.

Not all of the many persons who have owned the house actually lived in it. Among the owners were Levi Hughes, a prominent businessman and banker, and Helen Chauncey Bronson Hyde, the wife of Benjamin Talbot Babbitt Hyde for whom Hyde Memorial State Park is named. After being rented during the 1940s and 1950s by Dr. Polhemus, the house became known as the "Palace of Health."

Despite modernization, the Preston House retains much of its original design and remains an example of a once elegant age.

PRESTON HOUSE stairwell, showing the midstair window seat under the large lunette window.
*Vincent Foster, photographer*

*Portal* view of ARIAS DE QUIROS site.
*Laura Gilpin, photographer*

# Arias de Quiros Site

## East Palace Avenue

Diego Arias de Quiros, a native of Asturias, Spain, received this land from General de Vargas as a reward for his services in the reconquest of New Mexico in 1693. Arias was a member of the Cofradía de la Conquistadora and of the military Cofradía de San Miguel in Santa Fe. The land adjoined the eastern *torreón* of the PALACE OF THE GOVERNORS, ran east to the *cienega*, including the location of the present Coronado Building, and north to Nusbaum Street. It was sufficiently large to plant 2½ *fanegas* of wheat. Arias de Quiros died in 1738 and the property, which included a two-room house with

a *zaguán*, was sold by his widow in 1746 to Manuel Sánz de Garvizu, lieutenant of the Santa Fe presidio, for 300 *pesos* of silver marked by the mint of Mexico City. The original house on the property probably vanished long ago, and the land has been subdivided and built over, but one of the structures may date back to the eighteenth century.

In 1879 L. Bradford Prince, newly appointed territorial supreme court justice for New Mexico, purchased the western portion from Carmen Benavides de Roubidoux of Costilla County, Colorado. The house was described as "consisting of seven rooms and according to the old description, sixty-one vigas." Carmen was the widow of Antoine Roubidoux, famous French-Canadian trader and interpreter for General Kearny in 1846. Roubidoux first came to Santa Fe about 1823, became a naturalized citizen in 1829, and the next year was elected to the *Ayuntamiento*, town council. As he married Carmen Benavides in 1828, their occupancy of the house may have begun at that time. They no longer made New Mexico their home after the middle 1830s, and the residents of the house until the purchase by Prince are unknown.

The 109 East Palace structure, sometimes known as the Trujillo Plaza, will be remembered historically as the first office (1943) of the Manhattan Project.

The eastern section (111–119 East Palace) was the inheritance of Manuel G. Sena from his parents, Juan Estevan Sena and María del Rosario Alaríd. Manuel Sena and his wife, Concepción García, lost the land to the Spiegelberg family through foreclosure in 1878, and after a series of owners, this property was also conveyed to Mr. and Mrs. L. Bradford Prince in 1886.

After his term as chief justice, Prince was governor of New Mexico, 1889–93, president of the Historical Society of New Mexico, chancellor of the New Mexico Missionary District of the Episcopal Church for forty years, and author of several historical works.

During the Princes' residence, this house was the scene of many celebrated social events.

The 115 East Palace building was used as an AWVS Service club for enlisted men during the Second World War. Today, the series of buildings contains a restaurant, offices, and shops but preserves many architectural details of the Spanish, Mexican Republican, and U.S. Territorial periods.

One of several ARIAS DE QUIROS courtyards.
*Tony Perry, photographer*

ROSARIO CHAPEL, showing both old, left, and new entrances.
*Bart Durham, photographer*

# Rosario Chapel and Cemetery

## Paseo de Peralta and Guadalupe

This chapel was granted a building license by the bishop of Durango in 1806 and was completed in 1807. It was intended for the reception of the statue of La Conquistadora during the annual novena, when it was taken in procession from the Santa Fe *parroquia*, now replaced by ST. FRANCIS CATHEDRAL, to the place where General de Vargas, his troops, and colonists were encamped during the reconquest of Santa Fe in 1693. While the soldiers battled the Indians entrenched in the PALACE OF THE GOVERNORS, the women and children prayed for success to the statue of the patroness, La Conquistadora. De Vargas made a vow to have the procession repeated annually in thanksgiving for the success of his mission. After some lapses the procession has been held for many years on the first Sunday after

the Feast of Corpus Christi, when the statue is taken to Rosario Chapel for a novena of masses and then returned to the Cathedral.

Although de Vargas also vowed to build a sanctuary for the statue, he did not accomplish this. There is no documentary evidence that anything other than a temporary shrine was built at Rosario before 1807, despite the statements of some writers. This date is carved inside the old doorway, and the original corbels and choir loft remain in place. The painted altar screen by Pedro Antonio Fresquís, dated 1809, was planned to contain the statue of La Conquistadora in a central niche into which it fitted nicely. No other image was included; panels were of flowers on a rose field divided by marbleized pillars. Fresquís (1749–1831), born at

89

Santa Cruz, was the first known native New Mexico *santero*. At Our Lady of the Rosary of Las Truchas, he painted another altar screen and several *santos*. The *retablo* at Rosario Chapel was badly damaged by having wallpaper pasted on it in later years.

By 1914 the chapel was too small for attending crowds, and a large addition was built against the east wall of the nave, which was then opened. This changed the main axis of the chapel from north-south to east-west. The former entrance and sanctuary became transepts. In 1962 a new altar and altar screen were installed, the work of Eugenie Shonnard, a Santa Fe sculptor who studied with Auguste Rodin.

When the St. Francis Cathedral was completed, burials were no longer made in the Cathedral grounds, but at Rosario Cemetery. Many prominent Santa Fe residents, including the late Archbishop Edwin V. Byrne, have been buried there.

Original 1807 entrance to Rosario Chapel.
*James B. De Korne, photographer*

Main altar of Rosario Chapel, sculpted by Eugenie Shonnard, with La Conquistadora.
*Vincent Foster, photographer*

Painted side altar screen, 1809, Rosario Chapel.
*Vincent Foster, photographer*

# Ignacio de Roybal House

**Jacona, New Mexico (private residence)**

ROYBAL HOUSE, with traditional well house.
*Bart Durham, photographer*

One of the oldest residences in the Pojoaque Valley, the Ignacio de Roybal House is an excellent example of New Mexico's Spanish Colonial architecture. Situated south of the Rio Pojoaque at the east side of the Jacona plaza, it is a one-story, flat-roofed adobe structure with a T-shaped floor plan. The multilayered adobe brick walls of the house are covered by the traditional layer of soft plaster reinforced with bits of straw. Long *canales* protrude just below the firewall to drain the roof, while on the west a *portal* braced by log pillars and corbels shelters the kitchen, living room and study which are arranged in tandem. All the doors and windows of the house are topped by pedimented lintels characteristic of New Mexico's Territorial style. Heavy *vigas* support the ceilings.

Spanish land conveyances show a dwelling on this location in the mid-1750s but its nucleus may date from 1705 when Don Ignacio de Roybal y Torrado purchased the land to augment his adjoining holdings. A veteran of the de Vargas Reconquest of 1693, Roybal was one of New Mexico's leading citizens during the first half of the eighteenth century, holding municipal offices in Santa Fe and serving as High Sheriff of the Inquisition.

Roybal first acquired land in the Pojoaque Valley from his brother-in-law, Captain Jacinto Pelaez, who had received a large tract in the area north of Santa Fe after the 1696 uprising of the Pueblo Indians, when the Pueblo of Pojoaque was abandoned. In 1705 Roybal enlarged his holdings by trading "a good traveling horse" for lands that extended to the Rio Cuyamungue. It was on this part of the Jacona ranch that Don Ignacio and his wife, Doña Francisca Gomez Robledo, maintained their residence and raised their family of nine children.

In 1707 the abandoned Pojoaque Pueblo was reoccupied by member families who had been living elsewhere. At that time it became apparent that the property that Roybal had purchased two years before constituted an encroachment on Pojoaque land. The matter remained in dispute for over two centuries. Meanwhile, despite various conflicting legal actions and decisions involving separate parties, the Roybals and their relatives, along with others in similar situations, continued to hold their property by rights of adverse possession. Finally, on November 24, 1937, a patent was granted to Porfirio Roybal by the United States government for the land that includes the Ignacio de Roybal House.

Before the end of that year, the house and land were purchased from Porfirio Roybal by Jon Glidden and his wife. At that time Glidden was embarking upon a new career that was to lead to his becoming the very successful Western writer who wrote under the name of Peter Dawson.

At the time of its purchase by the Gliddens, the house had been haphazardly altered on the interior through makeshift modifications and permitted to deteriorate. Minimal maintenance, but virtually no real improvements, had been performed. With the assistance and advice of several people who had considerable experience with restoration of houses in the Pojoaque Valley, the Gliddens embarked on the restoration of their new home.

All the dirt floors were prepared for pine planks. In redoing the kitchen floor—the only wooden floor in the house—an infant burial was uncovered. The wood from this floor was used as sheathing in a hallway. The Gliddens installed considerable interior woodwork and did all of the wood finishing themselves.

The front door shown in the accompanying photograph was designed around a lock from the old Pojoaque Church, which had burned in the 1920s. The screen doors, also shown here, were designed by Mrs. Glidden, using willow saplings from the nearby irrigation ditch. The *latillas* in the bedroom ceiling were removed, scrubbed in lye water, and relaid.

Perez Roybal, later a county sheriff for many years, mixed the adobe plaster for the house. The plastering was done by Francisca Roybal, Porfirio's wife, with the help of neighbors.

In 1976 the Ignacio de Roybal House was placed on the New Mexico State Register of Cultural Properties in recognition of its historic importance.

Double door entry to ROYBAL HOUSE.
*Bart Durham, photographer*

Interior of the RUSH STUDIO, with *vigas* painted by the artist and showing a collection of her art and furnishings.
*Alan B. Stoker, photographer*

# Olive Rush Studio

**630 Canyon Road**

One of the few adobe houses remaining in Santa Fe that has not been covered with concrete stucco for preservation, the Olive Rush Studio is typical of those purchased by artists and writers who flocked to Santa Fe and Taos during the first two decades of this century. Drawn primarily by their wish to record on canvas or in words the life of the Indian and the beauty of the landscape, they found in New

Mexico a place that the artist Frederic Remington described in 1902 as having been overlooked by the "heavy-handed God of Progress."

When Olive Rush, internationally known Quaker artist, first came to Santa Fe in 1914 she was so impressed by the country that she returned six years later to make it her permanent home. At that time she bought this house, which had been in the Sena and Rodríguez families for several generations, and it has been kept in very much its original state ever since. Its thick adobe walls, deep side *portal*, and charming back garden are all typical of the period, although efforts to document the exact building date have been unsuccessful. In the early days there were no surveys, deeds were not always filed, and descriptions of property were often confusing and inaccurate, particularly in the CANYON ROAD area where landowners knew their own boundaries and respected those of their neighbors.

For many years this building has served as a meeting house for the Santa Fe Religious Society of Friends, of which the late Rush was a birthright member.

Exterior of the RUSH STUDIO, one of the few remaining mud-plastered buildings.
*Karl Kernberger, photographer*

RUSH STUDIO entrance *placita*.
*Karl Kernberger, photographer*

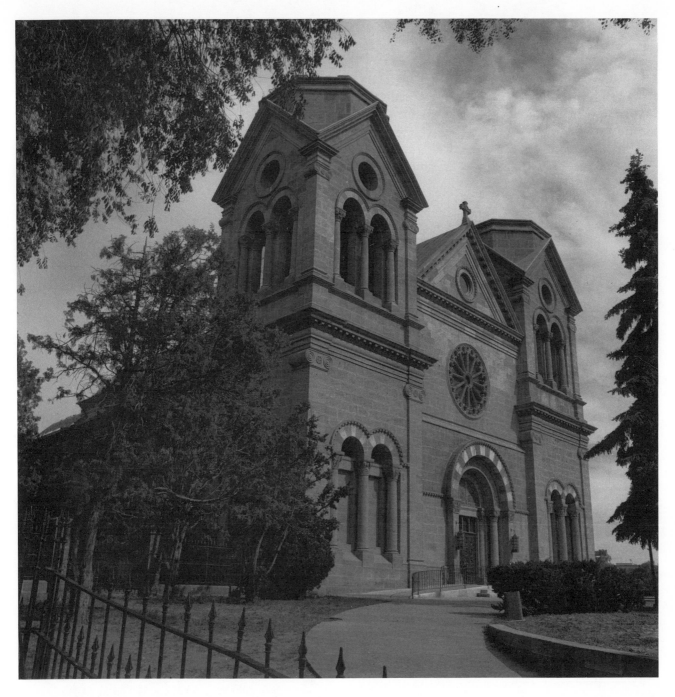

ST. FRANCIS CATHEDRAL, built by Bishop Lamy on the site of the original *parroquia*.
*Vincent Foster, photographer*

# St. Francis Cathedral

Bishop Jean Baptiste Lamy began construction of the stone St. Francis Cathedral in 1869 on the approximate site of earlier churches. Designed in the Romanesque style of Bishop Lamy's native Auvergne, the main building is architecturally foreign to Santa Fe's Spanish heritage and Indian back-

ground, except for the adobe chapel of Our Lady of the Rosary on the northeast that has survived from the earlier *parroquia*.

The first church near the site, with an adjoining *convento*, was built by Fray Alonso de Benavides about 1628, but was destroyed in the Pueblo Revolt of 1680. Its plan and exact location are unknown, but it probably stood immediately behind the present Cathedral, facing west.

In 1712 the adobe *parroquia*, which preceded the present Cathedral, was under construction. The chapel of Our Lady of the Rosary formed the northern portion of the transept and was dedicated to the small, sixteenth-century wooden statue of the Virgin known affectionately since the early Spanish period as La Conquistadora, Our Lady of the Conquest. Brought to Santa Fe by Benavides about 1625, the statue was originally known as Our Lady of the Assumption. It was taken to the El Paso region by the retreating Spaniards in 1680, and accompanied General Diego de Vargas back to Santa Fe during the reconquest of 1693 when, according to legend, its intervention on behalf of the Spaniards saved them from harm.

The *parroquia* was in ruinous condition by 1798 when it was restored, including La Conquistadora chapel, largely at the expense of Antonio José Ortiz, the wealthy Santa Fe citizen who was also responsible for major repairs to the CHAPEL OF SAN MIGUEL. Ortiz also subsidized the construction of a second chapel, dedicated to San José, on the south side of the *parroquia*. This chapel was demolished during recent remodeling.

The stone for the 1869 Cathedral came from local quarries at the Arroyo Sais, Lamy Junction, and the top of La Bajada Mesa. Much wider and half again as long as those of its predecessor, the walls of the new structure were built enclosing those of the *parroquia*, which remained in use until the nave was completed. The old adobe walls were then demolished and the rubble carted off. The choir loft and part of the walls of the chapel of Our Lady of the Rosary were removed, making the chapel shorter than it had been originally.

The Cathedral was never completed according to the original French plans that called for steeples rising to a height of 160 feet on each of its two towers. Supervised first by an American architect who proved unequal to the task, the work was continued by a French father-and-son team named Mouly. Italian stone cutters were also employed. The descendants of some are still living in Santa Fe.

La Conquistadora chapel, in continuous use since 1718 although reduced in size, is still the most interesting portion of St. Francis Cathedral. It contains the only stone sarcophagus of the Spanish period, in which repose the bones of two seventeenth-century friars who served at Picurís and Quarai and were especially revered by their Indian converts. Their remains were brought to Santa Fe for reburial in 1759 by Governor Marín del Valle. The existing altar is composed of two side altars made in Mexico in 1748 and sent to Santa Fe as gifts. The chapel is also the permanent home of La Conquistadora, the little wooden statue that has been the symbol of special religious devotion and Hispanic unity from colonial times to the present.

For the celebration of the first centenary of the dedication of the Cathedral, extensive renovations were completed in 1986 that included work in the sanctuary. A large, three-tiered wooden *reredos* decorated with paintings of fourteen American saints

La Conquistadora side chapel within ST. FRANCIS CATHEDRAL.
*The Historic Santa Fe Foundation photograph*

replaced the windows in the east wall. The central figure in the *reredos* is a 250-year-old wooden statue of St. Francis of Assisi taken from the *parroquia*. The cross of San Domiano was placed above the Cathedral's main altar.

Two new stained-glass windows from France with Eucharistic themes were installed in the remodeled Blessed Sacrament Chapel, which was partitioned off from the south transept to provide privacy for the parishioners.

The hollow metal doors at the Cathedral entrance were replaced with bronze-faced oak doors. They display sixteen bronze plaques depicting the history of the Catholic Church in New Mexico from 1539 to the present.

Wooden *reredos* depicting fourteen American saints was installed in 1989.
*Vincent Foster, photographer*

Two-story rear *portal* of St. Michael's Dormitory.
*James B. De Korne, photographer*

# St. Michael's Dormitory

## South of San Miguel Chapel

Erected in 1878 by the Brothers of the Christian Schools, this building was for many years the main structure of St. Michael's College. It was originally three stories high and was the highest and largest adobe building in Santa Fe. Typical late nineteenth-century details included a tower, porticos, galleries, and a mansard roof. Administration, class, and faculty rooms occupied the first two floors, while the third floor was used as a dormitory.

The Christian Brothers were brought to Santa Fe by Bishop Lamy in 1859 to establish a school for boys. For nearly twenty years, St. Michael's was housed in a much-remodeled single-story building. Funds to construct the new facility were raised by Brother Botulph, veteran educator and first director of the college, who went through the territory in 1877 seeking contributions. In addition to money and building materials, the record of donations listed

735 sheep, two young oxen, a heifer worth $8 and two goats valued at $1 each.

A disastrous fire in 1926 destroyed the tower and the third floor, which were not rebuilt. The appearance of the building was thus greatly altered, but the graceful two-story rear *portal* is one of the few remaining in Santa Fe. The French-style trim around the doors and windows and the original mansard roof were due to the influence of Bishop Lamy and the early Christian Brothers, all of whom were Frenchmen.

After 1947, when St. Michael's College (now The College of Santa Fe) was organized as a separate unit and moved to the southern part of town, this building served as the dormitory for St. Michael's High School. The property was sold by the Brothers to the state of New Mexico in 1965 and now houses state offices. It has been renamed the Lamy Building.

California Mission Revival-style SALMON-GREER HOUSE.
*Vincent Foster, photographer*

# Salmon-Greer House

## 505 Don Gaspar

This home of two prominent merchant families still stands in pleasant solitude at the busy corner of Don Gaspar Street and Paseo de Peralta. It was built in 1909 by the Nathan Salmons. Their daughter's family, the John Greers, moved into it in the 1930s.

The Salmon-Greer House was designed in the Mission Revival style, which originated in California in the 1890s. Now that its original red brick has been stuccoed white, it adheres more closely to the style today than it did when first built. The floor plan based on a center hall is not characteristic of the Mission style, however, the arcaded porch and "tile" roof (actually tin molded to imitate tile) have always left no doubt of its California Mission Revival inspiration.

Nathan Salmon immigrated to the United States in 1887 and came to Santa Fe in the 1890s. When he decided to build this house shortly after the turn of the century, his choice reflected the current fashion of using styles that evoked a Spanish Colonial past. Another example is the BRONSON M. CUTTING HOUSE built in 1910. The more regionally appropriate Spanish Pueblo Revival and Territorial Revival styles would soon come to dominate Santa Fe's architecture.

The house and exceptionally large garden are

99

surrounded by a wall, decorated with inset tiles and wrought iron arabesques, that was built in the 1920s after Salmon saw a similar wall in Mexico City.

Excluding a square, two-story addition at the rear, the main block of the house appears more horizontal than vertical, its two-story height muted by the low slope of the hipped roof and wide dormers. The exceptionally high sandstone foundation is tall enough to accommodate windows and encloses a full basement, an unusual feature in New Mexican houses of the period. Among the original furnishings was Nathan Salmon's pool table.

Located near the capitol, the house with its beautiful garden was both hospitable and convenient, and saw many gatherings of business and political leaders.

As the home of early and influential Santa Fe entrepreneurs, the Salmon-Greer House represents a significant chapter in the growth of the territory and is of interest as a local adaptation of the California Mission Revival style during its brief period of vogue in Santa Fe.

Fanciful wrought iron arabesques of the SALMON-GREER HOUSE wall.
*Vincent Foster, photographer*

SAN MIGUEL sanctuary, with eighteenth-century oil paintings and an earlier *estofado* sculpture of the church's patron saint.
*James B. De Korne, photographer*

# Chapel of San Miguel

## Old Santa Fe Trail and de Vargas Street

The original chapel of San Miguel had already been built in 1626 for the use of Indians from the BARRIO DE ANALCO when Custodian Fray Alonso de Benavides came to Santa Fe. No portion of this building is now visible. The Pueblo Revolt of 1680 began with the burning of San Miguel chapel. When de Vargas returned in 1693, he wrote that the walls were standing but repairs were not made, and in 1710 the chapel was completely rebuilt. Archaeological excavations in 1955 revealed the details of the rebuilding. The original sanctuary, which was square instead of angled, was uncovered together with its adobe altars and steps. The 1710 outer walls had been placed on separate foundations beside the older ones. The main beam of the choir loft is inscribed: "The Lord Marquess de la Peñuela had this built by his aide, Royal Ensign Don Agustín Flores de Vergara in the year 1710." The date was confirmed by tree-ring cores taken from that and other beams, corbels, and moldings in the chapel.

The expenses of rebuilding were borne by the military confraternity of San Miguel, to whose use the chapel was dedicated until the newer military chapel of LA CASTRENSE was erected on the PLAZA in 1760. The interior contains many good examples of eighteenth-century religious art in addition to its fine architectural woodwork. The gilded statue of St. Michael, the patron, is representative of *es-*

*tofado* sculpture at its peak in old Mexico. The statue was already in Santa Fe in 1709 when it was taken in procession over the entire colony to raise money, goods, or services for the rebuilding of the chapel.

Seven of the oil paintings on canvas were sent from Mexico about the middle of the eighteenth century. Before this time, the adobe sanctuary walls were painted with marbleized columns and flowering urns. The largest painting of St. Michael was the work of Captain Bernardo Miera y Pacheco, more famous for the maps of the Southwest which he made in the 1770s. He came to Santa Fe in 1756 and presumably did the painting before 1760, when the new military chapel became the fashionable one. Although Miera did not sign his work, it is inscribed with the name of the donor, Manuel Sanz de Garvizu, lieutenant of the Santa Fe presidio and owner of the ARIAS DE QUIROS property at the time.

The painted altar screen with its spiral pillars was made in 1798, as may be seen in the two inscriptions at the bottom stating that the screen was made and painted that year at the expense of Antonio José Ortiz. Ortiz, possibly the richest man in New Mexico at the time, was the most generous contributor to the construction of church buildings. The *retablo* was designed to set off the eight paintings on canvas and therefore had no images of holy persons painted on it, as did many altar screens in rural churches.

The bell, which formerly hung in the tower and is now to be seen in the gift shop of the chapel, was cast in Santa Fe by an itinerant bellcaster, Francisco Luján, in 1856. Defects in the sand-casting made the date appear to be 1356, which has led to some confusion about the age of the bell. However, eyewitnesses of the casting of the bell, and its later installation in San Miguel tower, were still alive in 1914 and left exact accounts of the process.

San Miguel's appearance has changed many times. The 1710 church had a small belfry and adobe battlements on the roof like a fortress church of sixteenth-century Mexico. In the early nineteenth century, it had a triple-tiered tower that collapsed in the 1870s, to be rebuilt in 1887 with a square tower and shuttered louvers, since removed. San Miguel served as a parish church for the south side of the river, but it has been neglected for long periods. In 1859 Bishop Lamy brought the Christian Brothers to Santa Fe to operate a school for boys. They bought the property and chapel, and managed a school and college until recently. When the school and college were moved, the property, except for the chapel, was acquired by the state of New Mexico for additional capital buildings.

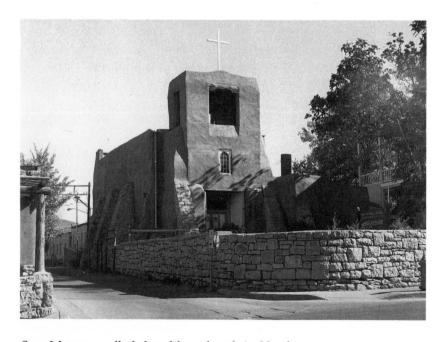

SAN MIGUEL, called the oldest church in North America.
*Bart Durham, photographer*

Virgin of Guadalupe altar screen, oil on canvas, signed Jose de Alzibar, 1783.
*James B. De Korne, photographer*

# Santuario de Guadalupe

### 100 Guadalupe Street

Archives of the archdiocese of Santa Fe show that a license to build this chapel was recorded on October 14, 1795. The date of its completion is uncertain, but it is probably the oldest shrine dedicated to the Virgin of Guadalupe that has survived in the United States. When first built, the chapel was typical of eighteenth-century New Mexico. It was adobe, cruciform, had a three-tiered tower, sand-cast copper bells, and a large painting on canvas of the Virgin of Guadalupe, which is signed on front and back: Jose de Alzibar, 1783. Alzibar was a popular painter of New Spain.

Antonio José Ortiz, the richest man in Santa Fe, in his will of January 31, 1805, left fifteen hundred sheep with whose products the costs of the annual function of Our Lady of Guadalupe were to be paid. Ortiz and his wife may well have given the painting by Alzibar to the chapel when it was completed since Ortiz was a merchant who made frequent trips to Mexico.

When the military chapel, LA CASTRENSE, was dismantled, the *vigas* and corbels from it were taken to the Guadalupe chapel. Cores from them give a tree-ring date of 1753. In 1856 an itinerant bell-caster, Francisco Luján, cast a bell in front of the old Santa Fe parish church that was then placed in the tower of the Guadalupe chapel. This bell was later sold. Its inscription read: Juan Sena y Da. Maria Manuela de Atocha-Santa Fe Agosto 21 de 1856. Sena and his wife were the donors of the bell.

When the railroad arrived in 1880, Bishop Lamy appointed Father de Fouri to be pastor for the newly arrived, non-Spanish-speaking Roman Catholics. Extensive remodeling in the neo-Gothic style took place on the interior, Gothic windows were cut in the walls, and a peaked shingle roof was added. In 1922 the church was again remodeled after a fire, this time in California Mission style instead of that of Franciscan New Mexico. After a new church was built next to it in 1961, the old chapel was neglected until recently, when it was repaired through efforts of members of the parish. The choir loft from LA CASTRENSE and the Alzibar painting, cleaned and restored in 1969 by Paraguayan scholar Dr. Estella Rodríguez Cubero, are still in place.

Deeded to the Guadalupe Historic Foundation in 1974, the Santuario interior was completely renovated by 1976. The restoration was additionally funded by federal and municipal grants, and by donations from private organizations and the general public. It is now open for tours, art exhibits, lectures, and theatrical and musical events that celebrate and preserve Hispanic arts and traditions.

South facade of SANTUARIO DE GUADALUPE, showing entrance bell tower, tile roof, and walled biblical herb garden.
*Vincent Foster, photographer*

SANTUARIO DE GUADALUPE, front facade.
*Bart Durham, photographer*

104

Stone quoin and window detailing evoke the early history of the SECOND WARD SCHOOL.
*Vincent Foster, photographer*

# Second Ward School

**312 Sandoval Street**

Constructed in 1886, the Second Ward School is situated south of the Santa Fe River next to the present New Mexico Employment Security Building. A one-story, hip-roofed structure now covered with brown stucco, it was the first building in Santa Fe erected specifically as a public school, an important step forward in the development of local education. The site on Hancock Street, as Sandoval was then known, was originally purchased by the county for a farmers' market, but that project was not particularly successful and was abandoned after a few years.

Little is known of the first years of the Second Ward School except that only students from the primary grades attended its two classrooms. In an early report regarding conditions in the school, Su-

perintendent James A. Wood noted that he had hung an old bell on top of the building at a cost of four dollars "from donations" and received a new flag from prominent Santa Feans, Mr. and Mrs. Thomas B. Catron. In the same report Wood also stated that, "We as teachers are endeavoring to create a sentiment among the pupils for regularity in attendance."

During the 1920s it became increasingly apparent that the two-room Second Ward School was unsuited to the needs of a growing community such as Santa Fe. In 1932 Alvord School on Hickox Street was opened and the old structure, which was then referred to as the Hancock Street School, was closed after more than forty-five years of service.

Central courtyard of SENA PLAZA.
*Laura Gilpin, photographer*

# Sena Plaza

### East Palace Avenue

The land on which Sena Plaza now stands was once part of the property granted to Captain Arias de Quiros by General Diego de Vargas, with whom he campaigned during the reconquest of New Mexico in 1693. By the will of Juan Nepomuceno Alaríd, dated 1844, this portion of the ARIAS DE QUIROS property passed to his sister, María del Rosario Alaríd, wife of Juan Estevan Sena, and thence to their son, José D. Sena, who was a major in the United States army during the Civil War.

At the time of Don José's marriage in 1864 to Doña Isabel Cabeza de Baca, daughter of an equally prominent Santa Fe family, the property included a *placita* to the west and a small adobe house, which eventually increased to become a hacienda containing thirty-three rooms. All of these were on the first floor except for the second-story ballroom added to the west side. This was reached, as it is today, by an outside stairway. After the territorial capitol burned on May 13, 1892, this ballroom served as a meeting place for the legislative assembly until it could be housed elsewhere.

The family of Don José, which included eleven children, lived on the south, east, and west sides of the inner patio, where guests were always welcomed with Spanish hospitality. A coach house, storerooms, a chicken house, and servants' quarters occupied space on the north. The well at the east and two front entrances remain in their original location, but a well at the west has been filled.

Upon the death of Major Sena and his wife, the land was divided into equal strips, 16½ *varas* in width, for the six surviving children. In 1927 these heirs deeded the property to Senator Bronson M. Cutting, Martha R. White, and Amelia E. White, who restored and remodeled the building for preservation. The original two-story portion at the west had been deeded to Dr. Frank E. Mera, who added it to the restoration project. The heirs reserved the right, however, to erect the family altar under the *portal* facing Palace Avenue for the annual Corpus Christi procession, and for many years thereafter

it was a colorful part of this religious celebration.

The second story on the eastern and northern portions of the building was added in 1927, when the property changed hands. This work was done under the supervision of William Penhallow Henderson, a well-known Santa Fe artist, designer, and builder. It is a classic example of how a historic building can be restored and reconstructed to adapt to modern business requirements while keeping the integrity of the original.

Because of the long, continuous *portal* in front of the Sena, Prince, and Trujillo buildings on this site, the inclusive name "Sena Plaza" is often given to the entire building complex. The above data refer only to the building and patio at its eastern end and not to those on the west.

SENA PLAZA, courtyard entrance.
*Todd Webb, photographer*

*Zaguán* entrance to SENA PLAZA *portal* and courtyard.
*Peter Dechert, photographer*

SHONNARD HOUSE, 1890.
*Vincent Foster, photographer*

# Eugenie Shonnard House

## 1411 Paseo de Peralta

The Shonnard House is one of two extant Santa Fe residences built by master carpenter Philip Hesch (HESCH HOUSE). It served as the home and studio of internationally known sculptor Eugenie Shonnard (1886–1978) from 1934 until her death.

The lot on which the house stands, and the three-room adobe structure at the rear, were purchased by Rosa Gallegos from Santa Fe merchant José Arban Ortiz and his wife in 1874. Rosa Gallegos and her husband, Bruno Romero, sold the property in 1890 to Nestora Lucero de Kirchner, the wife of August Kirchner, a merchant and druggist.

In 1890 Nestora contracted with Hesch for the construction of the house. Financial difficulties apparently beset the Kirchners, for construction liens were placed against the property and it was sold at public auction in 1892.

During the early decades of this century, the house was owned by local merchant Charles Kiesov and his wife, Emma.

Eugenie Shonnard had studied art in New York and in Paris with Auguste Rodin in the early 1900s. During her career she created many marble, granite, and bronze sculptures on commission. Her works were exhibited in leading galleries and are in the permanent collections of the Metropolitan Museum of Art and the Luxembourg Palace.

In 1927 an exhibit of her work at the Museum of New Mexico's Fine Arts Division brought Eugenie Shonnard to Santa Fe, where she settled permanently later that year. In 1934 she received the house as a wedding gift from her mother.

The Shonnard House is listed on the New Mexico State Register of Cultural Properties and on the National Register of Historic Places.

The 1880 adobe home of Willi Spiegelberg, member of an early prominent merchant family.
*Vincent Foster, photographer*

# Willi Spiegelberg House

## 237 East Palace Avenue

The Spiegelberg House commemorates an influential Jewish mercantile family. The first Spiegelberg to settle in Santa Fe, Solomon Jacob, arrived with the U.S. army that occupied New Mexico in 1846. During the next fifteen years, his five brothers, Levi, Elias, Emanuel, Lehman, and Willi, also migrated to New Mexico. The Spiegelberg brothers operated a store on the south side of the PLAZA and were involved in mining ventures, land speculation, construction enterprises, insurance, and banking. In addition, they served as sutlers and mail route contractors for several New Mexico military posts and Indian agencies.

The Spiegelberg House was built in 1880 by European artisans who had come to New Mexico because of the extensive building program of Archbishop Jean Baptiste Lamy. (The same craftsmen may also have built the FRANCISCA HINOJOS HOUSE at 355 East Palace Avenue, which is architecturally similar.) The house is adobe, but the woodwork is typically Territorial. Although most of the fourteen rooms have shallow, coal-burning fireplaces, the house was the first in Santa Fe to be equipped with gas pipes.

The second owners of the house were Dr. and Mrs. John Symington, who occupied it in 1888. Dr. Symington practiced medicine across the street at St. Vincent Sanatorium, operated by the Sisters of Charity. The house was sold in 1900 to another prominent merchant, Solomon Spitz. In 1963 the house was purchased by the present owners, who have restored it substantially to its original appearance.

The Spiegelberg House is listed on the State Register of Cultural Properties and on the National Register of Historic Places.

STONE WAREHOUSE facade.
*Vincent Foster, photographer*

# Stone Warehouse

### 316 Guadalupe Street

This building, erected about 1885, is probably the oldest stone commercial structure in Santa Fe. Originally constructed of rough, undressed stones to serve as a warehouse, the east side, which fronts on Guadalupe Street, was later faced with bricks and sandstone blocks to form a typical late nineteenth-century mercantile facade.

The building is located in the section south of the Santa Fe River designated during the late Spanish and Mexican periods as the Barrio de Guadalupe, since its residents were in the jurisdiction of the SANTUARIO DE GUADALUPE.

This *barrio*, in common with the BARRIO DE ANALCO that joined it on the east, was the district inhabited by the common soldiers and their families. In 1860 the land on which the store is now located belonged to the Tapia family. Several Tapias had been soldiers in the presidial company of Santa Fe during the Mexican period, as had their neighbor, José Salaices, who owned much of the adjoining property. Salaices sold his holdings shortly thereafter, and the new owners and the Tapias built their houses along Agua Fria and present Guadalupe streets so

that they formed a complex with a *placita* common to the various landowners.

Cesaria Tapia sold the southern part of her property to Frederick Schnepple, a merchant and shopkeeper, in 1880. He apparently erected the stone building to serve as a warehouse before conveying the property to merchant John Dendahl on June 28, 1886, since the deed of that transaction contains the first direct reference to the building. It specifies the real property sold as including a frame dwelling, stable, sheds, an adobe residence, and a stone storehouse, and states that the property adjoined the common *placita*. The storehouse also appears on the 1886 Hartman map.

For several years prior to the sale of the property by Dendahl to Alphonse Dockwiler in 1916, the building was used by Henry Krick, agent for Lemp's Key and Bottled Beer. Dockwiler owned the building for ten years before conveying it in 1926 to J. A. Hart, who used it as headquarters for the Coca Cola Bottling Company. Since that time it has housed several commercial ventures, including an electrical supply store and a gallery.

Street entry into *placita* of Tudesqui House.
*Alan K. Stoker, photographer*

# Roque Tudesqui House

## 129–135 East de Vargas Street (private residences)

Although its exact building date is unknown, this house and property in the Barrio de Analco was bought by Italian-born merchant Roque Tudesqui about 1839. Many of its adobe walls are more than three feet thick.

Tudesqui was a trader on the Santa Fe Trail who decided to make Santa Fe his home and acquired considerable property and business interests. The 1839 census listed him as "38 years old, single, trader." However, in 1842 he remedied that situation by marrying María Ignacia Larrañaga, descendant of a military surgeon who had come to Santa Fe in the 1770s.

In 1841 Tudesqui sold this property to Juan Nepomuceno Lopez and his wife, María Rita Sandoval, who owned other land in this *barrio*. Later owners were the mercantile firm of Ardinger & Rumley (who used it "as lodgings"), James S. Gray, Reuben Frank Green (the 1846 operator of the famous Exchange Hotel on the site of present La Fonda), and William L. Jones. In 1895 Jones divided the property and sold the western portion to Bertha L. Cartwright. His will, probated in 1899, designated the eastern section for the life tenancy of Elizabeth Bolander and, after her death, to the Church of the Holy Faith. The church came into possession in 1921 and the next year sold the property to Sophie Knapp. After a succession of owners, Marjorie Allen purchased the property during the 1950s.

Not only did Allen and her mother carefully maintain the venerable building, but they made the spacious back yard into a garden show place. In late spring a wisteria blooms in the front patio of the east part of the house. Nearly a century old, the trailing vines have grown high into the branches of an old tree.

After the tragic death of Allen in 1987, The Historic Santa Fe Foundation purchased the house from her heirs in accordance with her wish that the organization be given the right of first refusal.

Corner fireplace in the TUDESQUI HOUSE living room.
*Vincent Foster, photographer*

TUDESQUI HOUSE garden showing terraces, fruit trees, and back view of the house.
*Vincent Foster, photographer*

The 1851 faux-brick adobe TULLY HOUSE.
*Vincent Foster, photographer*

# Pinckney R. Tully House

## 136 Griffin Street at Grant Avenue

This attractive ten-room house is an outstanding example of Territorial architecture, and unlike most historic houses in the city, it has undergone no major exterior changes since its original nine rooms were built in 1851, except for the addition of a tenth room with bay window during the 1880s. The list of its owners and occupants reads like a nineteenth-century *Who's Who* of Santa Fe.

The property on which the house is located was purchased prior to 1851 by James Conklin, a French-Canadian trader who came to Santa Fe in the 1820s shortly after the opening of the Santa Fe Trail. In 1829 he married Juana Ortiz. The previous owner, José Albino Chacón, was a municipal judge and militia officer during the late days of Mexican rule. Conklin's son-in-law, Pinckney R. Tully, also a Santa

Fe trader, built the house fronting on "the road from the Plaza to Tesuque" in the summer of 1851. During the middle 1850s the Tully family moved to the Mesilla Valley, and Pinckney was a leading Confederate sympathizer during the Civil War. In 1863 he became a partner of Estevan Ochoa, pioneer freighter in southern Arizona, with headquarters in Tucson.

After Tully left Santa Fe, Conklin mortgaged the property to two other well-known traders: first to William S. Messervy, also secretary of the territory, and then to James T. Webb. In 1857 he deeded the house to another son-in-law, Oliver P. Hovey. Ten years earlier, Hovey had enlisted in Ceran St. Vrain's "mountain men militia company" to assist Colonel Sterling Price in crushing the Taos revolt of 1847.

113

Later that year, Hovey began publication of New Mexico's first English newspaper, *The Santa Fe Republican*, on a press which he had shipped from Missouri. In addition to being a journalist and Indian trader, Hovey was also a member of the territorial legislature. As a staunch Union man at the outbreak of the Civil War, he was commissioned Major General of the Second Regiment of Territorial Militia in 1861. Hovey used the property as security in financial dealings with such controversial men as the ex-priest, José Manuel Gallegos; Alexander M. Jackson, secretary of the territory; and William Pelham, first U.S. surveyor general for New Mexico, who had his office in this house. Both Jackson and Pelham were arrested as Confederates when Union forces reoccupied Santa Fe in April 1862.

Important Santa Feans who owned the property during the late 1800s were Attorney General William Breeden and Dr. Robert H. Longwill, both of whom were members of the "Santa Fe Ring," a group of leading citizens then dominating New Mexican affairs; Rufus J. Palen, long-time president of The First National Bank of Santa Fe; and Henry L. Waldo, chief justice of the supreme court, later solicitor for the Santa Fe Railroad.

During the twentieth century, the house was owned by such prominent citizens as Levi A. Hughes, businessman and banker; Mrs. James W. Raynolds, whose husband was at the time secretary of the territory; Grace Bowman, and her partner in the Avery-Bowman Abstract Company, Jennie Avery. Bowman converted a portion of the house into apartments, one of which was occupied in 1926 by New Mexico author Erna Fergusson.

In 1972 the Pinckney R. Tully House was threatened with demolition. By 1974 The Historic Santa Fe Foundation, aided by significant public support, had purchased it and begun the work of restoration. The architectural reproduction of the 1890s style included the unique feature of painting white rectangles on red plaster to duplicate the simulated brick exteriors that were popular at the time. A small portion of the original "brick" has been preserved and can be seen under the south *portal.*

The Tully House project was completed with the assistance of numerous contributions and government grants.

1974 restoration of the faux-brick detailing of Tully House. Note original painting on left.
*The Historic Santa Fe Foundation No. 254 photograph*

The UNITED STATES COURT HOUSE, built of native stone.
*Karl Kernberger, photographer*

# United States Court House

## South Federal Place

When this large building of native New Mexico stone was finally completed in 1889—thirty-six years after construction began—it was considered one of the most handsome, up-to-date structures in the city. Today it stands as one of the very few remaining unaltered examples in the Southwest of the imposing public buildings of that period, once common particularly throughout the Midwest. Although the architectural style is Greek Revival and not indigenous to this area, its unusual history, good proportions, and honest materials make it worthy of inclusion among the historic buildings of Santa Fe.

The land on which it was built was part of the public grounds acquired by the United States from the Mexican government under the 1848 Treaty of Guadalupe Hidalgo. Immediately after the territory of New Mexico had been organized in 1850, the U.S. Congress appropriated an inadequate $20,000 for the construction of a "capitol building." In 1854 another $50,000 was added, but these funds were exhausted after only one and a half stories had been built above the basement, and for the next twenty-five years the building stood without a roof and in a state of "increasing dilapidation."

An 1860 appropriation of $60,000 to complete the

115

building was never paid as a result of New Mexico's exemption from special war taxes during the Civil War.

Further attempts were made during the 1860s and 1870s to finish construction, as it was necessary to rent other space for the functions of the federal courts and territorial legislature. Among the appeals sent to Washington was one explaining the lack of competent workmen to cut the stone for the building, which was "of the hardest nature and very difficult to cut," and another that "all the tools to work with must be brought from the States" as no such equipment was available in New Mexico. The rough stone for the walls was quarried in the Hyde Park region of Santa Fe, and the dressed stone in Cerrillos, New Mexico.

Except for these appeals, the half-built structure, which was said to bear a striking resemblance to "the hulk of a coal barge," was neglected until the summer of 1883, when the grounds around the building were selected as a site of Santa Fe's so-called Tertio-Millennial celebration, promoted by several prominent citizens, including L. Bradford Prince and Arthur Boyle. The grounds were cleared and graded, the stone walls were given a tempo-rary roof, and an exterior stairway was built to the first floor, which was used to house out-of-town Indian participants during the six weeks the fair was in progress. They were advertised as practic-ing crafts and holding chicken pulls, races, tribal dances, and other ceremonials, and in one perfor-mance the Court House was used as the backdrop for a staged battle between the Indians and Coro-nado's forces. A racetrack about one-third of a mile long was laid out around the grounds, generally following the present Federal Place oval. Horse, mule, and burro races were held here, as were com-petitive drills by territorial cavalry units.

In May 1885 a simple stone monument to Kit Carson was erected at the main (south) entrance of the building by his comrades of the Grand Army of the Republic. It was unveiled in the presence of some 5,000 persons.

Several more years passed before work started again on the Court House, but it was finally com-pleted in 1889, together with the circular stone wall and iron fence around the federal grounds. An ad-dition at the north, in the same architectural style as the original building, was constructed in the years 1929–30.

"Canyon de Chelly," one of several murals by William Penhallow Henderson on the interior of the UNITED STATES COURT HOUSE.
*Vincent Foster, photographer*

The 1918 VIERRA HOUSE, showing *portal* and the second-story set-back, a design element encouraged by Vierra.
*Vincent Foster, photographer*

# Carlos Vierra House

## 1002 Old Pecos Trail (private residence)

A major spokesman for reviving the Spanish Pueblo style of architecture in Santa Fe, Carlos Vierra best demonstrated his architectural preferences in the residence he constructed at 1002 Old Pecos Trail. Following the arrival of the railroad in 1880, the traditional Spanish Pueblo style of architecture was being replaced with more "modern" architectural styles in Santa Fe and other New Mexico towns. The older buildings were systematically razed or extensively altered to conform to changing tastes. If it were not for Vierra and others like him who reversed this trend, the architectural character of Santa Fe would be very different today.

Carlos Vierra first came to New Mexico in 1904 in an effort to improve his failing health. After his recuperation, Vierra became associated with attorney Frank Springer, a member of the board of regents of the Museum of New Mexico and president of the managing board of the School of American Archaeology (which in 1917 became known as the School of American Research). Springer became Vierra's patron and helped him both by exerting influence on his behalf and by financial support.

By 1912 Vierra was a staff member of both the Museum of New Mexico and the School of American Archaeology and became involved with the restoration of the PALACE OF THE GOVERNORS under the supervision of archaeologist Jesse L. Nusbaum. This undertaking launched the revival of the Spanish Pueblo architectural style in Santa Fe.

In 1918 Vierra began construction of a home for himself and his wife, Ada Talbert Ogle. Knowing that the Vierras lacked sufficient building funds, Frank Springer gave them a life interest in a lot on the corner of Old Pecos Trail and Coronado Road. In July 1919 the Santa Fe *New Mexican* reported on Vierra's progress:

> One of the largest and in many ways most artistic houses is that which Carlos Vierra, the artist, is building. . . . The construction of his home began many months ago but this spring and summer it has made a mark on the landscape and is much admired. It is two stories high, in the Santa Fe style of which Mr. Vierra is an apostle, and is of adobe with various layers of brick. It promises to be "the last word" in original Santa Fe style houses with several sleeping porches. There are charming vigas and quaint fireplaces.

Carlos Vierra died in Santa Fe on December 20, 1937. His wife continued to live in the house until the early 1940s, when she moved to Kansas, and ownership of the property reverted to the Springer family.

Santa Feans are indebted to Carlos Vierra, as Paul A. F. Walter observed in an editorial published the day after Vierra's death:

> It was Vierra's insistence upon purity of style that saved Santa Fe from many an architectural monstrosity. . . . Up to the time of his death he guarded the integrity of the Pueblo and Spanish colonial architecture with a zeal often leading to heated controversy. That Santa Fe is not only a "City Different" but also a "City Beautiful" is more largely owing to him, perhaps, than to any other one individual.

Entry into Vierra House *placita*.
*Hope A. Curtis, photographer*

Interior *placita* and north entrance to VIGIL HOUSE.
*Karl Kernberger, photographer*

# Donaciano Vigil House

### 518 Alto Street (private residence)

In 1832 this house with its farmlands and orchard was the residence of minor city official Juan Cristóbal Vigil, his wife María Antonia Andrea Martínez, and his large family, among whom was a soldier son, Donaciano. It then apparently included the buildings on either side of the front portion, as Juan Cristóbal in his will dated May 31 of that year and María Antonia in her testament of May 26, 1834, described it as "composed of four parts." After the death of his mother, Donaciano bought out the other heirs and added still another section, probably on the south. Today, the buildings facing Alto Street have different owners, but the main part of the house, with its charming inner *placita*, is the private residence of the person responsible for its restoration. The doors and windows used in the restoration came from the original Loretto Academy in Santa Fe and are Territorial in style.

The house is of special historic value, in addition to its charm and antiquity, as the former residence of Donaciano Vigil, one of the most important military and political figures of his day. While Santa Fe was under Mexican rule, 1821 to 1846, he served first in the presidial company of Santa Fe and then commanded the company of San Miguel del Vado. He was also military secretary to Governor Manuel Armijo. After U.S. occupation in 1846, General Kearny appointed him secretary of the territory, and in January 1847 he became acting civil governor of New Mexico following the assassination of Governor Charles Bent. From 1848 to 1850 he continued as secretary of the territory and register of land titles.

In 1851 Donaciano led the opposition to the secular use of LA CASTRENSE by the U.S. government. As a member of the Santa Fe grand jury, he refused to take his place in the courtroom of the U.S. court of the first judicial district that had been located by Judge Grafton Baker within the church. His stand against violation of a consecrated structure where his own father was buried resulted in the removal of the court to the PALACE OF THE GOVERNORS. Some reports of the incident state that Judge Baker threatened to arrest Vigil but changed his mind when the townspeople and army personnel rallied to Vigil's support.

When this house served as the home of Donaciano Vigil and his wife, Doña Refugia Sánchez, its lands extended along the Río de Santa Fe and still contained the orchard mentioned in his parents' wills. At that time it was the scene of much civil and political activity, but in 1855 the Vigils retired to their ranch on the Pecos River, and in 1856 sold the property to Vicente García. They are buried in ROSARIO CEMETERY. In May 1969 the house was placed on the State Register of Cultural Properties and subsequently on the National Register of Historic Places.

VIGIL HOUSE *zaguán*.
*Alan K. Stoker, photographer*

Alto Street entrance to VIGIL HOUSE *zaguán*.
*Alan K. Stoker, photographer*

## Professor J. A. Wood House

Territorial-style entrance of the WOOD HOUSE.
*Vincent Foster, photographer*

### 511 Armijo Street (private residence)

The low adobe house with Territorial trim sits half-way up the slope on property that first appears on the records in 1860. In that year Bernardino Sais purchased it from Jose Sandoval and Rosario Sais de Sandoval for thirty *pesos*, four *reales* (about $35). In 1879 the price was $200 when it was bought by Abelerio Nuañez and his wife, Victoria Sanches de Nuañez. Then it was described as being "*. . . al lado norte este de Río y así al espaldo* [sic] *de la loma . . . una casa que constru de cuatro piesas* [sic] *con cuarenta y dos vigas,*" (on the northeast side of the River and thus at the shoulder of the hill . . . a house built of four rooms with forty-two *vigas*).

The Nuañez ownership, 1879–1883, may have corresponded with a significant enlargement of the house and its rather elaborate embellishment. From an original four rooms of approximately 1,300 square feet, the house grew to about 1,700 square feet with the addition of a two-room wing on the northwest.

Possibly at the same time, certainly in the late nineteenth century, the adobe received a fashionable sprucing up with new Territorial entrance and front window treatments, including a "store-bought" front door with arched panes over panels, side-lights with paneled bases, and a transom. Interior detail at the time was either perfectly plain or Territorial (a New Mexico adaptation of a Greek Revival). Some doorways were finished with molding-edged facings, for example, and the fireplaces had simple Greek Revival framing. The floor plan of the original house reflects Territorial ideas rather than traditional Spanish Colonial, as its four rooms were arranged not linearly, but in a cluster.

By June 1899 when James A. Wood bought it, the house was a suitable residence for the new superintendent of Santa Fe City Schools. A dapper gentleman who sported a derby, Wood's enthusiasms included bicycling and work with the Baptist church, as well as his professional endeavors. The latter were impressive, for while head of the Santa Fe system he reorganized the schools, planned the first high school building, improved old buildings, and helped obtain the Fort Marcy Reservation for the school system.

Fortunately for the continuity of architectural history in Santa Fe, the old Territorial adobe that was in the Wood family for more than seventy years has been carefully restored.

121

The double-wide entrance in the center *placita* of
EL ZAGUÁN.
*Karl Kernberger, photographer*

# El Zaguán

**545 Canyon Road (private residences)**

One of the architectural treasures of New Mexico, this rambling old hacienda and its garden stretch more than 300 feet along lower CANYON ROAD. Named El Zaguán because of its long covered corridor, running from the large garden at the west to an open patio at the east, the building now contains nineteen rooms that have been converted into private rental apartments of various sizes.

When it was bought in 1849 by James L. Johnson, a prominent merchant during the days of the Santa Fe Trail, it was of Spanish Pueblo style and consisted of two or three rooms, which can be identified by their four-foot-thick adobe walls. Johnson

came to New Mexico from Maryland at the age of twenty and later owned a general store on the northeast corner of the PLAZA. He added more rooms to his residence, with walls three feet thick, including a "chocolate room" where chocolate was ground and served each afternoon, a "treasure room" with barred windows where the family valuables were kept, a private chapel, and a semidetached room overlooking the west garden for his library, said to have been the largest in the territory. Architecturally, these later rooms were Territorial in style, which accounts for the brick coping on the roof. At one time the house contained twenty-four rooms, with servants' quarters across the street.

On the lower terrace behind the houses were orchards, a cornfield, and large corrals where freighters on the Santa Fe Trail kept their horses and oxen before making the return trip.

The large west garden (picture on page 126) was laid out by Adolph Bandelier, and its peony bushes, imported from China more than 100 years ago, are still flourishing. The two large horse chestnut trees, which were planted by Johnson, have become city landmarks.

As the home of Colonel and Mrs. James Baca, Johnson's grandson, the property was long known as the Baca Place, but in 1927 it passed out of the family. Threatened with demolition to make way for a modern apartment building, it was bought by Margretta S. Dietrich. A private girls' school known as Brownmoor was housed in the building during the early 1930s. Later, the house was converted into rental apartments without changing its exterior appearance. Even the old well still remains under the back *portal*.

After the owner's death in 1961, the building was again bought for preservation, this time by a corporation formed specifically for that purpose. In December 1979 The Historic Santa Fe Foundation acquired the last outstanding shares of that corporation, El Zaguán, Inc. One of the apartments now houses the Foundation office.

In 1960 the building was measured and recorded by the Historical American Buildings Survey for the Library of Congress in Washington.

EL ZAGUÁN from CANYON ROAD.
*Vincent Foster, photographer*

The handsome central *portal* that gives EL ZAGUÁN
its name.
*The Historic Santa Fe Foundation photograph*

# Glossary

acequia: irrigation ditch

acequia madre: (mother ditch) main irrigation ditch from which water is diverted into laterals

adobe: a mixture of dirt, sand, chopped straw, and water that can be molded into sun-dried building blocks or used as plaster

alacena: recessed cupboard

alcalde: municipal official during the Mexican period with authority similar to a justice of the peace

ayuntamiento: town council

baile: dance or ball

barrio: ward or district of a town

battered wall: a wall that recedes as it rises

camino: road

camino real: (royal road) maintained at government expense

canal: drain spout

casa: house

casa real: term used to identify government building

castrense: military chapel

cienega: marsh; marshy region; area of springs

cofradía: (confraternity) local church society approved by a bishop

convento: residence of a Franciscan friar

corbel: a carved, decorative piece of wood that tops a post and helps support a beam

estofado: type of sculpture or painting made by covering a surface with a whitewash of powdered gypsum (yeso) and then applying paint. A coat of gold leaf is finally added. The processes were often executed by different individuals.

fanega: measure of wheat and other grain equivalent to 1½–2½ bushels

farolito: (small lantern) a festive light made of a candle seated in sand in a paper bag

garita: sentry box or tower. La Garita, north of Santa Fe, was the traditional place of execution during the Mexican period.

genízaros: Indians who had been captured by nomadic tribes and had lost their identity, and were subsequently captured or ransomed by the Spaniards, or wandered into the settlements. They agreed to live in a Europeanized status, and settlements were granted to them.

hacienda: landed property or estate usually containing a sizable residence

jacal: wall construction of vertical posts chinked with adobe

kiva: Pueblo Indian ceremonial room

latilla: small peeled pole used in ceilings

luminaria: small pitch bonfire lighted for festive occasions

mayordomo de la acequia: supervisor of an irrigation ditch or ditch system

molina: mill

muralla: wall, usually for defensive purposes

oratorio: private chapel

parroquia: parish church as distinguished from a mission

peso: standard measure of currency considered the equivalent of a dollar

placita: small plaza or square serving a complex of buildings, or located in the center of a private home

plaza: public square

plaza mayor: the main town square, situated in the center of a settlement

político: politician

portal: long porch or portico with roof supported by vertical posts and corbels

presidio: permanent garrison of soldiers

pretil: defensive parapet on top of a building; firewall

puddled adobe: mud shaped by hand into long, low bands. As each band dried, another layer was added until a wall was formed.

raja: ax-split piece of cedar or spruce used for ceilings

rancho: ranch

reredos: altar screen

retablo: representation of a religious figure painted on a flat surface

rico: rich man

sala: reception room or drawing room

santero: local designer of santos

santo: image of a saint

*torreón:* defensive tower
*trastero:* hand-carved wooden cupboard
*vara:* measure of approximately 33 inches
*villa:* town or city in the Spanish Colonial period
  designated as a center of administration

*viga:* ceiling beam
*zaguán:* roofed space joining separate buildings or
  rooms

Bandelier Garden from the porch of EL ZAGUÁN,
with horse chestnut trees in bloom
(text on p. 123).
*The Historic Santa Fe Foundation photograph*

E. D. Smith
714 Walnut Court
No. 401
Darien, Illinois 60561